D0947545

Essential Computer Science

A Programmer's Guide to Foundational Concepts

Paul D. Crutcher
Neeraj Kumar Singh
Peter Tiegs

Apress®

Essential Computer Science: A Programmer's Guide to Foundational Concepts

Paul D. Crutcher
Welches, OR, USA

Neeraj Kumar Singh
Bangalore, Karnataka, India

Peter Tiegs
Hillsboro, OR, USA

ISBN-13 (pbk): 978-1-4842-7106-3
https://doi.org/10.1007/978-1-4842-7107-0

ISBN-13 (electronic): 978-1-4842-7107-0

Managing Director, Apress Media LLC: Welmoed Spahr
Acquisitions Editor: Susan McDermott
Development Editor: Laura Berendson
Coordinating Editor: Rita Fernando

Cover designed by eStudioCalamar

Cover image designed by Freepik (www.freepik.com)

Distributed to the book trade worldwide by Springer Science+Business Media New York, 1 New York Plaza, New York, NY 10004. Phone 1-800-SPRINGER, fax (201) 348-4505, e-mail orders-ny@springer-sbm.com, or visit www.springeronline.com. Apress Media, LLC is a California LLC and the sole member (owner) is Springer Science + Business Media Finance Inc (SSBM Finance Inc). SSBM Finance Inc is a **Delaware** corporation.

For information on translations, please e-mail booktranslations@springernature.com; for reprint, paperback, or audio rights, please e-mail bookpermissions@springernature.com.

Apress titles may be purchased in bulk for academic, corporate, or promotional use. eBook versions and licenses are also available for most titles. For more information, reference our Print and eBook Bulk Sales web page at http://www.apress.com/bulk-sales.

Any source code or other supplementary material referenced by the author in this book is available to readers on GitHub via the book's product page, located at www.apress.com/9781484271063. For more detailed information, please visit http://www.apress.com/source-code.

Printed on acid-free paper

To my wife, Lisa, for her unending support and encouragement; to my sons currently studying computer science, Kyle and Cameron, may this be a bit of inspiration for their journey in life; and to the memory of my father, Edwin Lee Crutcher, who passed away while I worked on this book. I love you, Dad!

—Paul

To my wife, Shilpi, for her unwavering support.

—Neeraj

To Karen, Jane, Josephine, Henri, and Jeanette, my family, for all of their support, patience, and encouragement.

—Peter

Table of Contents

About the Authors

Paul D. Crutcher is a senior principal engineer at Intel Corporation, managing the Platform Software Architecture team in the Client Computing Group (CCG). Paul has worked at Intel for more than 25 years and has also worked at two smaller software companies. Paul has a degree in computer science, with expertise spanning software development, architecture, integration, and validation based on systems engineering best practices in multiple areas. He holds several patents and has multiple papers and presentations to his credit.

Neeraj Kumar Singh is a principal engineer at Intel with more than 15 years of system software and platform design experience. His areas of expertise are hardware/software (HW/SW) codesign, system/platform architecture, and system software design and development. Neeraj is the lead author of two other books, *System on Chip Interfaces for Low Power Design* and *Industrial System Engineering for Drones: A Guide with Best Practices for Designing*, in addition to many other papers and presentations.

ABOUT THE AUTHORS

 **Peter Tiegs** is a principal engineer at Intel with around 20 years of software experience. Inside Intel, he often consults on DevOps topics such as build automation and source code branching. Over the last decade, Peter evangelized continuous integration and delivery as well as agile practices at Intel. Peter has written software at all levels of the stack from embedded C code to Vue.js. His programming language of choice is Python.

About the Contributors

Chockalingam Arumugam is a system software architect with expertise in design, development, and delivery of software solutions that work across OSs. He holds a master's degree in software systems from Birla Institute of Technology and a bachelor's degree in electronics and communications from Anna University. He is a hands-on technologist on OS-agnostic software development and has over 12 years of experience in the industry. In recent years, he has been specializing in cloud-based telemetry solutions.

Through his career, he has worked on a broad set of domains, including device drivers, firmware/platform services, desktop/universal applications, web applications, and services. He specializes in the areas of Platform Health Analytics, Windows crash decode, and thermal and power management debug and has led multiple engagements in these areas. These solutions are used extensively in the industry for client platform validation and debug. He is currently based out of Bangalore, India, and works at Intel Corporation.

Prashant Dewan is a principal engineer at Intel and is very passionate about computer security. At Intel, he has worked on multiple security technologies and has filed 100+ patents in the area of computer security. He has a master's and doctorate in computer science from Arizona State University.

About the Technical Reviewer

 **Kenneth Knowlson** is a senior principal engineer in the Client Computing Group (CCG) division at Intel. He leads a group of principal engineers in the Analytics and DevOps subgroup, within CCG, leading the organization's strategic and technical direction in these dynamic areas. Prior to joining CCG, Ken invented the processes and procedures for "pre-silicon" (Pre-Si) software and system development at Intel. The Pre-Si initiative is focused on accelerating time to market by shifting SW and FW development "left," before Si is available, enabling products to come to market much faster than they would otherwise. Pre-Si uses technologies like Virtual Platform, FPGA, and System-Level Emulation to approximate the final Si-based product. Ken also has a long history at Intel creating and delivering consumer-connected media products streaming media space.

Ken holds bachelor's degrees in mathematics and physics from the University of California Santa Cruz. Ken enjoys swimming and running and also holds black belts in taekwondo and hapkido, although he no longer practices.

Acknowledgments

We would like to express gratitude to the people who helped us through this book, some of them directly and many others indirectly. It's impossible to not risk missing someone, but we will attempt anyway.

First and foremost, we would like to sincerely thank our technical reviewer, Ken Knowlson, for meticulous reviews; it helped the book significantly. Thank you, Ken!

We would like to acknowledge Prashant Dewan for writing Chapter 6 and Chockalingam A. for his help on Chapter 4 of the book.

Thank you so much Rita Fernando, Susan McDermott, and all of the Apress publishing team for the outstanding work, help, guidance, and support; you have gone the extra mile to make the book what it is.

Above all, we thank our family and friends for their understanding and support and for being continuous sources of encouragement.

Introduction

According to code.org, there are 500,000 open programming positions available in the United States alone – compared to an annual crop of just 50,000 graduating computer science majors. The US Department of Labor predicted there will be 1.4 million computer science jobs by 2020, however, only enough people to fill roughly 30% of these jobs. To bridge the gap, many people not formally trained in computer science are employed in programming jobs. While they are able to start programming and coding quickly, it often takes them time to acquire the necessary understanding and gain the requisite skills to become an efficient computer engineer or advanced developer.

The goal of the book is to provide the essential computer science concepts and skills necessary to develop a sound understanding of the field. It focuses on the foundational and fundamental concepts upon which expertise in specific areas can be developed, including computer architecture, programming language, algorithm and data structure, operating systems, computer networks, distributed systems, security, and more.

This is a must-read for computer programmers lacking formal education in computer science. Secondarily, it is a refresher for all, including people having formal education in computer science as well as anyone looking to develop a general understanding of computer science fundamentals.

Overall, we authors have attempted to make it as lucid as possible, so people with limited or even no background in computer science can pick up the book and go through the journey to develop a good understanding of computer science. We're excited to have you on board.

CHAPTER 1

Fundamentals of a Computer System

There are many resources online to get you started programming, but if you don't have training in computer science, there are certain fundamental concepts that you may not have learned yet that will help you avoid getting frustrated, such as choosing the wrong programming language for the task at hand or feeling overwhelmed. We wrote this book to help you understand computer science basics, whether you already started programming or you are just getting started. We will touch on the topics someone with a computer science degree learns above and beyond the semantics and syntax of a programming language. In this first chapter, we will cover a brief history and evolution of a computer system and the fundamentals of how it operates. We will cover some low-level computer architecture and programming concepts in this chapter, but subsequent chapters will cover higher-level programming concepts that make it much easier to program the computer.

von Neumann Architecture

You've probably heard stories about computers the size of an entire room in the 1940s into the 1970s, built with thousands of vacuum tubes, relays, resistors, capacitors, and other components. Using these various

© Paul D. Crutcher, Neeraj Kumar Singh, and Peter Tiegs 2021
P. D. Crutcher et al., *Essential Computer Science*,
https://doi.org/10.1007/978-1-4842-7107-0_1

components, scientists invented the concept of gates, buffers, and flip-flops, the standard building blocks of electronic circuits today. In the 1970s, Intel invented the first general-purpose microprocessor, called the 8088, that IBM used to make the first PC that was small enough for personal use. Despite the continuous advancements that have made it possible to shrink the microprocessor, as you'll see, the core elements of today's desktop or laptop computer are consistent with the first computers designed in the 1940s!

In 1945, John von Neumann documented the primary elements of a computer in the "First Draft of a Report on the EDVAC" based on the work he was doing for the government. EDVAC stands for Electronic Discrete Variable Automatic Computer, which was the successor to the Electronic Numerical Integrator and Computer (ENIAC), the first general-purpose computer developed during World War II to compute ballistic firing tables. EDVAC was designed to do more general calculations than calculating ballistic firing tables. As depicted in Figure 1-1, von Neumann described five subdivisions of the system: central arithmetic and central control (C), main memory (M), input (I), output (O), and recording medium (R). These five components and how they interact is still the standard architecture of most computers today.

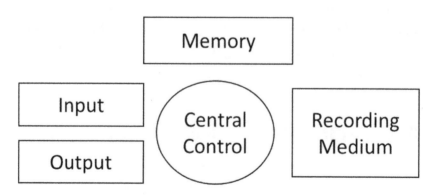

Figure 1-1. Primary Architecture Elements of a Computer

In his paper, von Neumann called the central arithmetic and control unit the central control organ and the combination of central control and main memory as corresponding to associative neurons. Even today, people refer to the central processing unit, or CPU, as the "brain" of the computer. Don't be fooled, though, because a computer based on this architecture does exactly what it is programmed to do, nothing more and nothing less. Most often the difficulties we encounter when programming computers are due to the complex nature of how your code depends on code written by other people (e.g., the operating system), combined with your ability to understand the nuances of the programming language you're using. Despite what a lot of people might think, there's no magic to how a computer works, but it can be complicated!

CPU: Fetch, Decode, Execute, and Store

The CPU's job is to fetch, decode, execute, and store the results of instructions. There are many improvements that have been invented to do it as efficiently as possible, but in the end, the CPU repeats this cycle over and over until you tell it to stop or remove power. How this cycle works is important to understand as it will help you debug multi-threaded programs and code for multicore or multiprocessor systems.

Note   Threads are a mechanism used to simulate executing a set of instructions in parallel (at the same time), whereas multiple cores in the same system actually do execute instructions in parallel.

The basic blocks of a CPU are shown in Figure 1-2. The CPU needs a clock that sends an electric pulse at a regular interval, called a frequency. The frequency of the clock dictates how fast the CPU can execute its internal logic. The control unit drives the fetch, decode, execute, and store function of the processor. The arithmetic and logic unit, or ALU, performs math operations and digital logic operations like AND, OR, XOR, and so on. The CPU has an internal memory unit for registers and one or more high-speed memory caches to store data proactively pulled in from main memory.

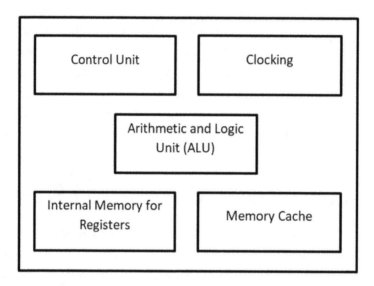

Figure 1-2. *Basic Blocks Inside a CPU*

Fetch

The CPU fetches instructions from memory using addresses. Consider your home's mailbox; it has an address and, if it's anything like my mailbox, contains junk mail and a letter from my mom, if I'm lucky. Like the mail in your mailbox, instructions sit in memory at a specific address. Your mailbox is probably not much bigger than a shoebox, so it has a limit to how much mail the mail carrier can put into it. Computer memory is similar in that each address location has a specific size. This is an important concept to grasp because much of computer programming has to do with data and instructions stored at an address in memory, the size of the memory location, and so on.

When the CPU turns on, it starts executing instructions from a specific location as specified by the default value of its instruction pointer. The instruction pointer is a special memory location, called a register, that stores the memory address of the next instruction.

Here's a simple example of instructions in memory that add two numbers together:

Address	Instruction	Human-Readable Instruction
200	B80A000000	MOV EAX,10
205	BB0A000000	MOV EBX,10
20A	01D8	ADD EAX,EBX

The first column is the address in memory where the instruction is stored, the second column is the instruction itself, and the third column is the human-readable version of the instruction. The address and instruction numbers are in hexadecimal format. Hexadecimal is a base 16 number system, which means a digit can be 0–F, not just 0–9 as with the decimal system. The address of the first instruction is 200, and the instruction is "mov eax,10," which means "move the number 10 into the EAX register." B8 represents "move something into EAX," and 0A000000 is the value. Hexadecimal digit A is a 10 in decimal, but you might wonder why it's in that particular position.

It turns out that CPUs work with ones and zeros, which we call binary. The number 10 in binary is 1010. B8 is 10111000 in binary, so the instruction B80A000000 in binary would be 1011 1000 0000 1010 0000 0000 0000 0000 0000. Can you imagine having to read binary numbers? Yikes!

In this binary format, a single digit is called a "bit." A group of 8 bits is called a "byte." This means the maximum value of a byte would be 1111 1111, which is 255 in decimal and FF in hexadecimal. A word is 2 bytes, which is 16 bits. In this example, the "MOV EAX" instruction uses a byte for the instruction and then 4 words for the data. If you do the math, 4 words is 8 bytes, which is 32 bits. But if you are specifying the number 10 (or 0A in hexadecimal) to be moved into the EAX register, why is it 0A000000? Wouldn't that be 167,772,160 in decimal? It would, but it turns out processors don't expect numbers to be stored in memory that way.

```
bit          0 or 1
byte         8 bits
word         2 bytes = 16 bits
dword        2 words = 4 bytes = 32 bits
```

Most CPUs expect the lower byte of the word to be before the upper byte of the word in memory. A human would write the number 10 as a hexadecimal word like this: 000A. The first byte, 00, would be considered the most significant byte; and the second byte, 0A, would be the least significant. The first byte is more significant than the second byte because it's the larger part of the number. For example, in the hexadecimal word 0102, the first byte 01 is the "most significant" byte. In this case, it represents the number 256 (0100 in hexadecimal is 256). The second 02 byte represents the number 2, so the decimal value of the hexadecimal word 0102 is 258. Now, let's look at the "MOV EAX,10" instruction as a stream of bytes in memory:

```
200:  B8     <- Instruction (MOV EAX)
201:  0A     <- Least significant byte of 1st word
202:  00     <- Most significant byte of 1st word
203:  00     <- Least significant byte of 2nd word
204:  00     <- Most significant byte of 2nd word
205:  ??     <- Start of next instruction
```

The instruction is a single byte, and then it expects 4 bytes for the data, or 2 words, also called a "double word" (programmers use DWORD for short). A double word, then, is 32 bits. If you are adding a hexadecimal number that requires 32 bits, like 0D0C0B0A, it will be in this order in memory: 0A0B0C0D. This is called "little-endian." If the most significant byte is first, it's called "big-endian." Most CPUs use "little-endian," but in some cases data may be written in "big-endian" byte order when sent between devices, for instance, over a network, so it's good to understand the byte order you're dealing with.

For this example, the CPU's instruction pointer starts at address 200. The CPU will fetch the instruction from address 200 and advance the instruction pointer to the location of the next instruction, which in this case is address 205.

The examples we've been studying so far have been using decimal, binary, and hexadecimal number conventions. Sometimes it is hard to tell what type of number is being used. For example, 10 in decimal is 2 in binary and 16 in hexadecimal. We need to use a mechanism so that it is easy to tell which number system is being used. The rest of this book will use the following notation:

> Decimal: No modifier. Example: 10

> Hexadecimal: Starts with 0x or ends in h. Example: 0x10 or 10h

> Binary: Ends in b. Example: 10b

Instruction Set Architecture

Instructions are defined per a specification, called instruction set architecture, or ISA. There are two primary approaches to instruction set architecture that have evolved over time: complex instruction sets and reduced instruction sets. A system built with a complex instruction set is called a complex instruction set computer, abbreviated as CISC. Conversely, a system built with a reduced instruction set is referred to as a reduced instruction set computer, abbreviated as RISC. A reduced instruction set is an optimized set of instructions that the CPU can execute quickly, maybe in a single cycle, and typically involves fewer memory accesses.

Complex instructions will do more work in a single instruction and take as much time to execute as needed. These are used as guiding principles when designing the instruction set, but they also have a profound impact on the microarchitecture of the CPU. Microarchitecture is how the instruction set is implemented. There are multiple microarchitectures that support the same ISA, for example, both Intel and AMD (Advanced Micro Devices) make processors that support the x86 ISA, but they have a different implementation, or microarchitecture. Because they implement the same ISA, the CPU can run the exact same programs as they were compiled and assembled into binary format. If the ISA isn't the same, you have to recompile and assemble your program to use it on a different CPU.

Note   A compiler and an assembler are special programs that take code written by humans and convert it into instructions for a CPU that supports a specific instruction set architecture (ISA).

Whether it is complex or reduced, the instruction set will have instructions for doing arithmetic, moving data between memory locations (registers or main memory), controlling the flow of execution, and more. We will use examples based on the x86 ISA to understand how the CPU decodes and executes instructions in the following sections.

Registers

CPUs have special memory locations called registers. Registers are used to store values in the CPU that help it execute instructions without having to refer back to main memory. The CPU will also store results of operations in registers. This enables you to instruct the CPU to do calculations between registers and avoid excess memory accesses. Table 1-1 is the original x86 ISA base register set.

Table 1-1. *x86 Base Register Set*

| | 64 bits | 32 bits | 16 bits(8086) | |
	(x86_64)	(x86)	8 bits	8 bits
Accumulator	RAX	EAX	AX	
			AH	AL
Base register	RBX	EBX	BX	
			BH	BL
Counter	RCX	ECX	CX	
			CH	CL
Data	RDX	EDX	DX	
			DH	DL
Base pointer	RBP	EBP	BP	
				BPL
Source index	RSI	ESI	SI	
				SIL
Destination index	RDI	EDI	DI	
				DIL
Stack pointer	RSP	ESP	SP	
				SPL
General purpose	R8-R15	R8D-R15D	R8W-R15W	
				R8B-R15B

It's important to understand how the registers are used by the CPU for the given ISA. For example, the 32-bit counter, in this case ECX, will be automatically decremented by the loop instruction. Another example is the stack pointer where you can directly manipulate it, but it's modified by many other instructions (we will explore the concept of a stack later in this chapter).

The x86 register set has evolved over time and is meant to be backward compatible with older versions of x86 CPUs. You can see the progression from the original 16-bit processor to 32-bit and the now more common 64-bit memory address sizes. As the memory address size increased, so did the register size, and new names were given to allow using the different register sizes with the appropriate instructions. Even when in 64-bit mode, the 32-bit register names enable programs written for 32 bits to run on 64-bit machines.

A typical ISA will have multiple register sets. For example, x86 has a floating-point register set and another register set for handling large data sets. The popular ARM architecture also has multiple register sets. The register set and the ISA go hand in hand!

Decode, Execute, and Store

Decoding is when the CPU interprets the instruction and transfers the data needed to execute the instruction into the CPU to prepare to execute the instruction.

Instructions are formatted in a particular way to enable efficient decoding. The instruction format specifies the opcode (the operation to be performed), the operands (the registers or data needed for the operation), and the addressing mode. The number and order of the operands depends on the instruction addressing mode as follows:

Register Direct: Both operands are registers:

```
ADD EAX, EAX
```

Register Indirect: Both operands are registers, but one contains the address where the operand is stored in memory:

```
MOV ECX, [EBX]
```

Immediate: The operand is included immediately after the instruction in memory:

```
ADD EAX, 10
```

Indexed: The address is calculated using a base address plus an index, which can be another register:

```
MOV AL,  [ESI+0x401000]
MOV EAX, [EBX+EDI]
```

The CPU control unit decodes the instruction and then, based on the addressing scheme, moves data from memory into the appropriate registers. At this point, the instruction is ready, and the control unit drives the ALU to do its work. For example, ADD EAX, 10 will add the number 10 to the current value of the EAX register and store the result in the EAX register.

The ALU can support typical math instructions like add (ADD), multiply (MUL), and divide (DIV) for integer numbers. The original arithmetic unit doesn't handle floating-point numbers directly. For example, when you divide a number using the DIV instruction, you put the dividend in EAX and the divisor in ECX and then issue the divide instruction:

```
MOV EDX, 0
MOV EAX, 13
MOV ECX, 2
DIV ECX
```

Since 13 is not an even number, there will be a remainder. The instruction deals with integers only, so the quotient, 6, is stored in EAX, and the remainder, 1, is stored in EDX. ECX will still be 2. You can use other registers for the divisor, but the quotient and remainder will be stored in EAX and EDX. In 16-bit mode, they are stored in AX and DX, and in 8-bit mode, this pattern breaks and the quotient is stored in AL with the remainder in AH.

Just like division has special handling for remainders, addition and subtraction have special handling for carrying and borrowing. For example, a binary number is either 0 or 1. The number 2 is represented as 10b in binary. When you add two bits together (1b + 1b), a carry occurs. This is easily represented digitally by an XOR logic gate and an AND logic gate. A logic gate is a set of transistors that perform logical operations on binary inputs. Figure 1-3 shows how the XOR and the AND gates are wired together to form a half adder circuit. The output of an XOR gate is "one or the other but not both," so it will be 0 if both inputs are 1. The output of an AND gate is 1 only if both inputs are 1. The output of the AND gate is used to set the carry bit for the add operation.

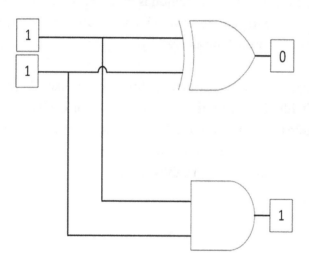

Figure 1-3. *Half Adder Circuit*

The ALU uses many different combinations of logic gates to implement the various instructions. In addition, the ALU also supports logic operations such as OR and AND, shifting bits, comparing, incrementing, decrementing, and more. We're just scratching the surface here, so if you're interested in more, we encourage you to study the ISA for your processor.

Controlling the Flow

A very important instruction is one that tells the CPU to start executing instructions from a different location, which is typically referred to as a "jump" instruction. You can program the CPU to perform calculations and then jump (change the instruction pointer) to a different location in memory based on the outcome of the calculations. This technique is used to perform a loop operation. In the following example, we will initialize the ECX counter register to 4 and the ESI index register to 0. Then we will increment the ESI register and call the LOOP instruction. The LOOP instruction has a special relationship with the ECX register. It will automatically decrement the register by one and, if it is greater than zero, jump to the specified location:

Address	Instruction	Human-Readable Instruction
0x0200	0xB904000000	MOV ECX,0x4
0x0205	0xBE00000000	MOV ESI,0x0
0x020A	0x46	INC ESI
0x020B	0xE2FD	LOOP 0x020A

Let's look at a slightly more complex example. Suppose you have two lists of numbers and you want to add them together and store the result somewhere else in memory:

List 1		List 2		List 3 (results)	
Address	Data	Address	Data	Address	Data
0x401000	01	0x402000	04	0x403000	00
0x401001	02	0x402001	03	0x403001	00
0x401002	03	0x402002	02	0x403002	00
0x401004	04	0x402003	01	0x403003	00

The following instructions add a number from List 1 to the corresponding number in List 2 and put the result in List 3. Again, we will use the ECX as a counter, so we initialize it to 4 since there are four elements in each list. Next, we initialize our source index register (ESI) and destination index register (EDI) to zero. Starting at address 0x0214, we move a byte from the first list into the AL register and a byte from the second list into the AH register. Next, starting at address 0x0220, we move one byte into our destination and then add the other byte to that same location. ESI is added to the address, and then the data located at that calculated address is moved into the AL register. Since we are adding ESI and EDI to the addresses, we increment both of them with the INC instruction before the LOOP instruction. The LOOP instruction automatically decrements ECX and jumps to address 0x214 as long as ECX is greater than zero. There are several other conditional loops and jump instructions that enable you to control program flow in a variety of ways:

Address	Instruction	Human-Readable Instruction
0x0205	0xB904000000	MOV ECX,0x4
0x020A	0xBE00000000	MOV ESI,0x0
0x020F	0xBF00000000	MOV EDI,0x0
0x0214	0x8A8600104000	MOV AL,[ESI+0x401000]
0x021A	0x8AA600204000	MOV AH,[ESI+0x402000]
0x0220	0x888700304000	MOV [EDI+0x403000],AL
0x0226	0x00A700304000	ADD [EDI +0x403000],AH
0x022C	0x46	INC ESI
0x022D	0x47	INC EDI
0x022E	0xE2E4	LOOP 0x0214

What if you needed to do this operation often? It would be of help if you could put this set of instructions in your program and jump to it from other parts of your program whenever you need to add two lists of numbers together, right? You would need to pass information to this code for the location of the two lists in memory, how many numbers are in the lists, and another memory location to store the results. Also, when the code is done, you need to tell the processor to return to the location it came from so it can continue execution instructions. We call this a function or routine, and thankfully the processor has special instructions and registers to keep track of the input to the function and where to jump to when the function is done doing its work. These special instructions store the needed information on the stack.

The Stack

The stack works on a Last In, First Out (LIFO) principle. Imagine a card game between two people sitting at a table. There are just a few simple rules. First, if there are no cards on the table, you can put a card on the table. If there's a card on the table, you must put the next card on top of the existing card, or stack them. Second, if either of you wants to take a card from the table, you have to take the card from the top of the stack. Thus, the last card put on the top of the stack is always the first one to come off the stack of cards. Of course, we're talking about computers, not people, so in a computer, the table is memory, the people are functions of your program, and the cards are data being passed back and forth. To make it more interesting, some CPUs require that the table is upside down!

For the x86 ISA, there are two instructions to work with the stack: PUSH and POP. There's also a special register called the extended stack pointer (ESP). The x86 stack always starts at a high memory address. As data is pushed onto the stack, the ESP decrements to the next address. When the pop instruction is executed, the ESP increments to reveal the previous item on the stack. Here is an empty 32-bit stack with ESP set to the address of the first available position:

Address	Data (DWORD)	ESP
0x01000000	0x00000000	0x01000000
0x00FFFFFC	0x00000000	
0x00FFFFF8	0x00000000	
0x00FFFFF4	0x00000000	

Let's push a value onto the stack and look at the result:

```
MOV   EAX, 10
PUSH  EAX
```

This is what the stack will look like and the value of the ESP register:

Address	Data (DWORD)	ESP
0x01000000	0x00000000	
0x00FFFFFC	0x0A000000	0x00FFFFFC
0x00FFFFF8	0x00000000	
0x00FFFFF4	0x00000000	

Notice anything? The value is actually stored in the next available spot, not the current location ESP was referring to! The push instruction decrements the address in the ESP register by 4, and then it stores the value at the location. The POP instruction does the opposite; it moves the value at the current address in the ESP register and then increments the ESP register by 4. If we do POP EAX, which means "take the value on the stack and put it in EAX," the stack will look like this in 32-bit mode:

Address	Data (DWORD)	ESP
0x01000000	0x00000000	0x01000000
0x00FFFFFC	0x0A000000	
0x00FFFFF8	0x00000000	
0x00FFFFF4	0x00000000	

The ESP register is now back to 0x01000000; however, the 0A value is still sitting at location 0x00FFFFFC! The POP instruction doesn't touch the data; it just copies it to the register you specify and changes the address value stored in ESP. However, you can't count on that data staying there as the next push command will overwrite it.

Now that we know how the stack pointer works, let's look at calling the routine we talked about earlier that adds the elements of two lists of numbers and stores the result in memory. Our routine needs the address of the two lists of numbers and the address where to store the results. It also needs to know the number of items in these lists, so let's push these items onto the stack:

Address	Instruction	Human-Readable Instruction
0x0200	0x6800104000	PUSH DWORD 0x401000
0x0205	0x6800204000	PUSH DWORD 0x402000
0x020A	0x6800304000	PUSH DWORD 0x403000
0x020F	0x6A04	PUSH BYTE +0x4

We use the DWORD and BYTE modifiers as hints to the compiler how to treat the numbers. We will cover compiling, linking, and loading in the next chapter. We also need to push an address on the stack so the routine knows where to tell the processor to return to when it is done and then jump to our routine. It turns out that the CALL instruction does this for us, so now we just need to call our routine, which is at address 0x024C in this example:

```
0x0211   0xE836000000      CALL 0x024C
0x0216   ;address of next instruction
```

Now the stack looks like this:

Address	Data (DWORD)	ESP
0x01000000	0x0401000	+16
0x00FFFFFC	0x0402000	+12
0x00FFFFF8	0x0403000	+8
0x00FFFFF4	0x0000004	+4
0x00FFFFF0	0x0000216	0x00FFFFF0

We can reference the parameters on the stack in relation to the current stack pointer. The beginning of our routine will use this technique to put the number of bytes in the lists into ECX, the destination for the results into EDI, the address of the second list of numbers in EBX, and the address of the first list of numbers in EDX. Then, we will do add the numbers together from the two lists and store them at the location stored in EDI. The code has changed a bit because we're using registers in a slightly different way, but it has the same outcome. Note that the ret instruction will use the address at ESP to jump to address 216 to continue executing the next instruction after the call to our routine:

```
0x024C   0x8B4C2404        MOV ECX,[ESP+4]
0x0250   0x8B7C2408        MOV EDI,[ESP+8]
0x0254   0x8B5C240C        MOV EBX,[ESP+12]
0x0258   0x8B542410        MOV EDX,[ESP+16]
```

```
0x025C    0xB800000000         MOV  EAX,0x0
0x0261    0xBE00000000         MOV  ESI,0x0

0x0266    0x8A0432             MOV  AL,[EDX+ESI]
0x0269    0x8A2433             MOV  AH,[EBX+ESI]
0x026C    0x00E0               ADD  AL,AH
0x026E    0x8807               MOV  [EDI],AL
0x0270    0x46                 INC  ESI
0x0271    0x47                 INC  EDI
0x0272    0xE2F2               LOOP 0x266

0x0274    0xC3                 RET
```

Our routine is simpler than the first list addition example; it doesn't need to use any temporary variables to get its job done. But if we did need temporary variables, there's a way to use the stack to store those variables so that you do not have to allocate them in memory and then have to remember to free that memory. If you use the stack, when your function returns, the stack pointer is adjusted appropriately. It's like a free scratch space for storing information. The way you accomplish this is to simply add the amount of space you want to allocate to the stack pointer, like this:

```
ADD    ESP, 24
```

One problem, though, is as routines call other routines (so-called subroutines), the stack will grow. The stack pointer will continue to grow downward as you push items onto it and call other functions. Within your routine, you need some way to reference your local variables. We use the EBP register, also called the base pointer, to save the value of ESP before we change it. There's a trick, though, because the routine that called our routine may also be using the base pointer to keep track of its local variable space. To avoid any issues, we push the current base pointer, set the base pointer to the current stack pointer, and then move the stack pointer, like this:

19

```
PUSH   EBP              ;save current base pointer
MOV    EBP, ESP         ;set base pointer to ESP
ADD    ESP, 24          ;move ESP down the stack
```

The area on the stack we use for this purpose is called the "stack frame." To reference this space, we can now subtract from the base pointer, EBP. For example, to initialize three locations on this space, you could do this:

```
MOV [EBP-4], 1
MOV [EBP-8], 2
MOV [EBP-12],4
```

Now we can reference those locations throughout our routine. When we exit our routine, we need to do some cleanup before calling the return function. Basically, we need to restore the stack pointer and then pop the EBP register off the stack to restore the stack frame to what our caller expected:

```
MOV ESP, EBP
POP EBP
RET
```

Remember how we pushed parameters on the stack before calling our function? We definitely want to clean those up. That can be done either by our routine using the RET (short for "return" to the caller) instruction, or we can expect the caller to clean up the stack. This is referred to as the "calling convention" for a routine. It's important to understand the calling convention that the code you are calling uses, and you should pick a consistent calling convention when you write code. Luckily, higher-level programing languages do this for us, but as we write assembly code to work with those higher-level languages, we need to follow those language conventions.

Instruction Pipeline

CPUs are designed to fetch, decode, and execute instructions as efficiently as possible. The circuitry of the CPU is designed in stages that can run in parallel, called parallel execution units. For example, when the CPU is performing the second stage of an instruction, it can start executing the next instruction's first phase. This allows the CPU to use all of its circuitry and execute instructions faster. The stages of executing an instruction are referred to as a pipeline.

A simple five-stage pipeline would have stages for fetching (F), decoding (D), executing (E), accessing memory (M), and writing to a register (R). Here are instructions executing without a pipeline:

T1	T2	T3	T4	T5	T6	T7	T8	T9	T10
F1	D1	E1	M1	R1					
					F2	D2	E2	M2	R2

The first row is time (T1–T10), the second row is the first instruction, and the third row is the second instruction. In this example, we can't fetch the second instruction until the first instruction completes all five stages:

Utilizing parallel stages in the pipeline, we can start fetching the second instruction after the first one moves to the second stage. This will enable the CPU to greatly decrease the amount of time it takes to execute the two instructions. Instead of ten steps, the instructions are done in only six steps, as follows:

T1	T2	T3	T4	T5	T6	T7	T8	T9	T10
F1	D1	E1	M1	R1					
	F2	D2	E2	M2	R2				

There are instances where the pipeline will not work well, for example, when the next instruction is relying on the result from a previous instruction. This is called a data hazard. If you're writing code in assembly language, you need to consider how you're using registers to ensure that these hazards are avoided. For higher-level languages, the compiler and assembler will optimize the machine language to ensure the pipeline is executing efficiently to get the best performance out of the processor.

Modern processors have a deep pipeline consisting of over 30 stages! They also use very fast internal memory called a cache to prefetch instructions and data and even execute instructions proactively by predicting the control flow.

Flynn's Taxonomy

Let's revisit the code we wrote to add the values of two lists of numbers. In that example, we were using the add instruction repeatedly on the data in memory. Each instruction was executed against a single piece of data. What if you could tell the processor to execute the add instruction on all of that data with a single instruction? Well, you can. It's called a single instruction, multiple data (SIMD) operation. In 1966, Michael J. Flynn proposed a taxonomy for the different ways that instructions operate on data.

Flynn defined a taxonomy in 1966 to classify parallel computing scenarios. In a parallel computing environment, you have multiple independent processors that can execute concurrently. Today, CPUs have multiple cores that can execute tasks in parallel, so they can execute parallel instructions. Flynn defined four classes, or scenarios:

Single instruction, single data (SISD)	Single instruction, multiple data (SIMD)
Multiple instruction, single data (MISD)	Multiple instruction, multiple data (MIMD)

We've been focusing on SISD, single instruction, single data, which is typical in a single-processor scenario. Let's look at our example of adding two lists of numbers together. The two lists of numbers are multiple data inputs, and it turns out there are instructions in the x86 instruction set that support multiple data inputs, or SIMD instructions as defined by Flynn. It's kind of interesting how it works. We will use the x86 PADDB instruction to add the values of both lists together in one shot. PADDB stands for "add packed integers." To use the PADDB instruction, you need to "pack" the data into a register using the MOVDQU instruction. MOVDQU stands for "move aligned double quadword." A double quadword is 128 bits ($2 \times 4 \times 16$) and is also referred to as an "OWORD." If you remember, our previous example used lists that had 4 bytes. If we increase those to hold 16 bytes, then we have 128 bits. We can "pack" those 128 bits of contiguous data into a 128-bit register using the MOVDQU instruction, use PADDB to do the addition in one instruction, and then move the result to the destination passed in on the stack as follows:

```
0x00000256   0x8B7C2404         MOV EDI,[RSP+4]
0x0000025A   0x8B5C2408         MOV EBX,[RSP+8]
0x0000025E   0x8B54240C         MOV EDX,[RSP+12]
0x00000262   0xF30F6F02         MOVDQU XMM0, OWORD [RDX]
0x00000266   0xF30F6F0B         MOVDQU XMM1, OWORD [RBX]
0x0000026A   0x660FFCC1         PADDB XMM0,XMM1
0x0000026E   0xF30F7F07         MOVDQU OWORD [RDI],XMM0
0x00000272   0xC3               RET
```

Using the PADDB instruction, we've removed the loop entirely! Packing your data into the XMM registers is the trick that makes it work. This implies that these instructions have limitations as to the amount of data you can pack and add at a time, so if the data set is large, you would still have to write a loop to complete the operation, but in the end it should be faster.

Multiple instruction, multiple data, or MIMD, is the case where you have multiple CPUs or CPU cores operating on multiple data streams at once. This is a typical multiprocessor scenario that happens often in today's seemingly single-processor systems. Most CPUs today have multiple cores built into them that can truly execute instructions in parallel. Most of the coordination of running programs on different cores in parallel is handled by the operating system. As a programmer, you write a program, and within that program if you want to execute multiple instructions concurrently on different CPUs, you create execution threads for those instructions with some help from the operating system.

Multiple instruction, single data (MISD) is a less common technique. A good example of MISD would be a fault-tolerant system where you may have processors run a known algorithm on the same data set. If the results don't match, the system knows one of the processors is malfunctioning, at which point it can stop using it and let humans know to replace it!

Main Memory and Secondary Storage

We've covered how the CPU fetches information from memory using addresses and how it decodes and executes instructions with help from special memory locations called registers. We also now know that information in memory is stored in byte-sized chunks (8 bits per byte) and that the CPU keeps track of the next instruction using an instruction pointer. To do its job effectively, the CPU must be able to access any location in memory quickly, which means the main memory must support random access. We call this type of memory "random access memory," or RAM. The main memory must be very fast and is implemented using electronic circuits consisting of capacitors and transistors that work together to store bits. Electronic circuits can only save information while they have power, so that type of memory is called "volatile memory." Therefore, a computer system also needs "non-volatile memory" that will save instructions when there's no power. This type of memory is called secondary storage.

Originally, instructions were encoded on punch cards that were fed by hand into memory. This was very cumbersome! Magnetic tape was originally invented to store audio in the late 1800s and further refined in the early 1900s. In 1950, the first tape recorder was created for storing digital information to be used by a computer. Information on a reel of magnetic tape could not be accessed randomly; instead, it had to be accessed from beginning to end, or sequentially. The tape drive is connected to the computer in a way that the computer can send the drive commands to start reading data from the tape and store it in a particular location in memory. After the instructions from the tape are loaded into memory, the CPU instruction pointer is set to start reading those instructions. This was better than punch cards, but still relatively slow, especially as the number of instructions and data used to run a program increased.

Researchers invented the "hard drive" to provide random access to instructions and data. Hard drives store data on magnetic disks housed in a special container. The disks spin at a high rate, and the mechanism to read the data is on an arm that moves left and right across the surface of the disk to read the data. This provided a cheaper and faster way to read programs from secondary storage into the much faster main memory.

Floppy disks are another type of magnetic media invented after tape. The advantage of a floppy disk was that it could be inserted into a drive that had a head that moved left and right while the disk was spinning to read blocks of data in a more random fashion (but still much, much slower than RAM). They were called floppy drives because they were somewhat flexible when not inserted into the drive.

Secondary storage technology has continued to evolve from high-density CD ROM, which is read and written to using a laser, to solid-state drives (SSDs) that have no moving parts at all. The evolution will continue with the advent of persistent memory that has the potential to be an alternative for main memory that does not lose its content when power is removed or lost. Imagine the implications of a system where the main memory is persistent and instructions no longer have to be moved from secondary storage to main memory before the CPU starts its fetch, decode, and execute cycle.

Input and Output (I/O)

We've talked about how the CPU needs to load the instructions from secondary storage into main memory. But how is that actually done? In modern computers, devices are connected to the same address bus as the CPU and main memory, as depicted in Figure 1-4. This enables CPU instructions to use memory addresses to perform input and output (I/O) operations with devices, which is called "memory-mapped I/O (MMIO)."

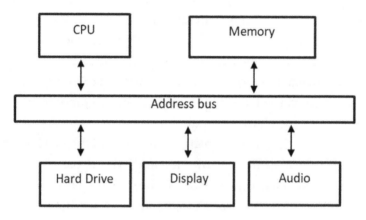

Figure 1-4. *Devices Connected to the Address Bus*

In early x86 processors, there were input and output instructions that read and wrote to I/O port addresses. Using other CPU instructions with the I/O port addresses would reference main memory, not the intended device. The only way to interact with the device was by using input and output instructions to load data into CPU registers and then execute instructions using those registers as operands. With memory-mapped I/O, you can simply use the address location for the device as the operand for any CPU instruction. The input and output instructions still exist in the x86 ISA, but aren't used except by the operating system and some common device drivers.

Through these memory accesses, the CPU can set values that the device interprets as commands. A common scenario is the CPU telling the device to transfer data into main memory, for example, having a hard drive transfer data from its disk to main memory, which is called direct memory access, or DMA. After telling a device to initiate direct memory access, the CPU is free to execute other instructions.

When a device completes its operation, it will let the CPU know it is done through an interrupt, which is a signal connected to the CPU that the device raises or lowers to get the CPU's attention. When the CPU receives the signal, it can stop executing instructions and switch to a special routine that takes care of the interrupt.

Summary

In this chapter, we learned about the fundamentals of a computer system:

- von Neumann Architecture: Central arithmetic and central control (C), main memory (M), input (I), output (O), and recording medium (R)

- Operation of a CPU: Fetch, decode, execute, and store

- Instruction set architecture and register sets

- Controlling the flow of execution and using the stack to implement routines

- Classifying parallel instruction and data using Flynn's taxonomy

- Understanding the difference between main memory and secondary storage

- Input and Output: Memory-mapped I/O and interrupts

Now that we have a basic understanding and hopefully appreciation of computer fundamentals, we can move on to Chapter 2.

References and Further Reading

- The ENIAC Story: https://web.archive.org/web/20110814181522/http://ftp.arl.mil/~mike/comphist/eniac-story.html

- Intel 8088 Microprocessor Family: www.cpu-world.com/CPUs/8088/

- "First Draft of a Report on the EDVAC": https://web.mit.edu/STS.035/www/PDFs/edvac.pdf

- History of Magnetic Tape: https://history-computer.com/ModernComputer/Basis/tape.html

- Introduction to Dynamic Random Access Memory: www.allaboutcircuits.com/technical-articles/introduction-to-dram-dynamic-random-access-memory/

- John L. Patterson, David A. Hennessy. *Computer Organization and Design: The Hardware/Software Interface.* Elsevier Science Ltd, 2007

- Intel 64 and IA-32 Architectures Software Developer Manuals: https://software.intel.com/content/www/us/en/develop/articles/intel-sdm.html

- ARM Developer Documentation: https://developer.arm.com/documentation

CHAPTER 2

Programming

In Chapter 1, we learned how the CPU fetches, decodes, and executes instructions and that those instructions sit on a persistent storage device until the CPU is turned on and transfers them to main memory. Of course, someone has to write the instructions in the first place, which we call "programming." So simply put, programming is the act of writing instructions for a computer to do some specific task. In this chapter, we will explore the different types of programming languages you can use, along with the advancements that have been developed over the years to make programming easier.

One of the most interesting aspects of computer science and software in general is how we are continuously inventing new programming languages. In the end, they are all converted to machine language appropriate for the ISA of a given CPU, but how this process is done varies. For example, in some cases the program is converted to machine language once. In other cases, the program may be converted every time it is about to be executed, in which case you need a program that does the conversion on the fly.

Deciding which programming language to use can be daunting when you look at the landscape of possibilities, and it's not always a black-and-white decision; often it comes down to personal preference.

Let's jump into the fundamentals of programming languages so you have a grounding in the basic concepts that are shared by almost all languages. There are entire books written about a single programming language, so we will touch on the basics and give you some good references for learning more.

© Paul D. Crutcher, Neeraj Kumar Singh, and Peter Tiegs 2021
P. D. Crutcher et al., *Essential Computer Science*,
https://doi.org/10.1007/978-1-4842-7107-0_2

Programming Language Fundamentals

It is possible to program a computer using the computer's native machine language. However, machine language is essentially a stream of binary numbers, which are difficult to read and extremely difficult to write. Listing 2-1 shows the machine language in hexadecimal format for a simple program. Can you tell what it's doing?

Listing 2-1. Machine Language for a Simple Program

Address	Instruction
00000098	B800000000
0000009D	B904000000
000000A2	BE00000000
000000A7	BF00000000
000000AC	6AF5
000000AE	E800000000
000000B3	6A00
000000B5	6800000000
000000BA	6A0C
000000BC	6800000000
000000C1	50
000000C2	E800000000
000000C7	6A00
000000C9	E800000000

No? That's not surprising! Obviously, we need a better way to program the computer, and that's where programming languages come into play. One of the first languages developed is called "assembly language." Assembly language is very close to machine language in terms of the instructions and syntax, so it is referred to as a "low-level" language.

Hello, World!

When you are learning a new programming language, it's common practice to write a program that prints "Hello, World" to the screen. This will enable you to understand the minimal amount of work you have to do to get the program to compile and output a message. Knowing how to output a message from your program is important because you may need to print messages from your program to help you debug it when it isn't working as intended. Let's look at printing "Hello, World" using assembly language in Listing 2-2.

Listing 2-2. "Hello, World" Using Assembly Language

```
STD_OUTPUT_HANDLE equ -11
NULL    equ 0

global  main
extern ExitProcess, GetStdHandle, WriteConsoleA

section .data
hello db "Hello, World", 0
hellol equ $ - hello

section .bss
dummy   resd 1

section .text
main:
        mov eax, 0
        mov ecx, 4
        mov esi, 0
        mov edi, 0

        push    STD_OUTPUT_HANDLE
        call    GetStdHandle
```

```
push    NULL
push    dummy
push    hellol
push    hello
push    eax
call    WriteConsoleA

push NULL
call ExitProcess
```

There's a lot going on in this example! You can see it uses a variable to represent a memory location (e.g., "hello"), specifies blocks of data (e.g., "section .data") and code (e.g., "section .text"), uses a label to represent the memory address of the start of the program (e.g., "main:"), and also leverages Windows operating system routines (e.g., "GetStdHandle," "WriteConsoleA," "ExitProcess"). There's also a section called "section .bss" where you declare variables that should be initialized to 0. This is obviously easier to read than raw machine language, as you can see, but it is structured in a particular way. Can you guess why that is?

Since the example isn't in machine language, the CPU can't execute the instructions directly. We need a special program called a compiler to convert the assembly language code into machine language.

Compile, Link, and Load

Unlike the machine language example that was dumped from memory, the assembly language example is text that you must save to storage as a file. The instructions in the file need to be converted to machine language and put into memory so the CPU can execute them. As depicted in Figure 2-1, this process is typically broken down into three phases: compile, link, and load.

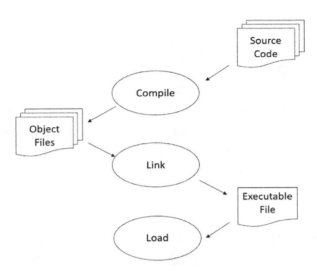

Figure 2-1. *Compile, Link, Load*

A compiler is a program that handles the task of taking the assembly instructions and converting them to machine language. The compiler verifies the syntax of the code relative to the language it is written in and generates machine language instructions for the CPU it will execute on. Much of the syntax in the assembly language example is there for the sake of the compiler so it can generate the appropriate machine code, for example, having to distinguish between data and code using "section .data" and "section .text," respectively. The compiler output will contain the values for global variables that are initialized to specific values (like "hello"), the code, a list of variables that should be initialized to 0, and references to functions that the compiler expects to come from some other source, like the output from another compiler or from the operating system. The binary files that the compiler generates are called object files. In Linux, object files have a ".o" extension, while Microsoft Windows object files have a ".obj" file extension.

A program called a linker takes multiple compiled object files and puts them together to create an executable program that can be loaded by a particular operating system. The linker's job is to make sure all the references in the object files are resolved before generating the executable program. It's common to get errors when linking a program typically indicating an incorrect or missing reference to a function or variable that you expected to import from some other source.

The ability to link object files from different sources together is powerful because it enables us to share and reuse code modules. When you create code that you want to reuse in multiple programs, you can have the compiler generate the object file and then use that object file when linking to other programs. We call this type of code a "static library." You can use different programming languages to generate them as long as the machine language they generate is compatible. For example, you could have two languages with a complier for each; the compilers need to use compatible mechanisms for passing parameters to functions on the stack so the code in their object files can call functions in other object files.

Static libraries are great for reusing code, but they have one drawback. If you update a static library because you've added functionality or fixed a problem in the code, you need to recreate the executable file for all the programs you've written that use that static library. Dynamic libraries were invented to fix this problem. You need to use special operating system calls to load dynamic libraries instead of linking the machine code directly into your program. This means you can update the dynamic library without having to recompile your original program – as long as the interfaces to the functions don't change! For now, just know that there are two types of libraries and that using dynamic libraries is a powerful, yet tricky, mechanism for reusing code.

Operating systems, like programming languages, are designed to make it easier to write programs. In the assembly language example, there are routines you can call to do work for you, like writing information to the console using the Microsoft Windows `WriteConsoleA` function. Another service the operating system provides is loading and executing your program. The operating system needs to know a few things about your program, like which part of it holds data (variables and default values), which part has instructions, and which instruction should be executed first. It will then put the data and instructions in memory and update the instructions to use appropriate memory locations. The operating system has a special program called a "loader" that handles this process. The loader expects the program to be stored as a file on a media device, like a hard drive, in a specific format, called the "executable file format." There are several executable file formats that have been developed over time, such as the Executable and Linkable Format (ELF), which is used by Linux (and many other operating systems). Microsoft Windows uses the Portable Executable (PE) format.

Separating the process into compiling, linking, loading, and executing phases is very flexible. For example, you could write compilers for many different languages that target the same linker. The compiler focuses on converting the intermediate instruction format to different types of instruction set architectures. It can also optimize the instructions for those specific architectures and create specific executable file formats. Having a program that has a specific output format that another program can work with is a very important concept in programming. Imagine how much more work it would be if every time someone came up with a new programming language, they had to write the compiler and linker and the executable file format, as well as load it and execute it! By breaking this process up into steps, it saves a lot of time and enables sharing of code between programs.

High-Level Languages

Let's compare our "Hello, World" assembly language example to an example written in the relatively old but popular "C" language. C became popular in the 1980s after Brian Kernighan and Dennis Ritchie published their edition of C in 1978. Their version included the standard input/output library, additional data types, and compound assignment operators. The following sample in Listing 2-3 is a simple "Hello, World" program in C, and as you can see, it is very different than assembly language!

Listing 2-3. "Hello, World" in the C Programming Language

```
#include <stdio.h>
int main() {
   printf("Hello, World!");
   return 0;
}
```

There are special keywords that you use so that the compiler can do its job. For example, the "#include" keyword tells the compiler to include another file, in this case "stdio.h," which is the C standard input/output library header file. Header files are used separate from the code files (which typically end in .c for the C language). They allow the compiler to understand how to call functions in other libraries without having to look at the code itself. The header file lists the names and parameters for functions that are available for use from the code file (as well as variable names and macro definitions). The brackets "<" and ">" tell the compiler to look for that file outside of the current folder by using the "include path," which is an operating system environment variable that we won't cover here. Every executable program in C must have a function called "main." Brackets ("{", "}") are used to group lines of code together. "printf" is a function that is defined in "stdio.h" that prints data to the screen. Parameters to the printf function are specified inside parentheses. A semicolon is used to specify the end of a string of commands.

The use of parentheses, brackets, and semicolons is all part of the C language syntax. The syntax is the rules for combining language-specific symbols in the correct order that the compiler will be able to understand.

Remember, the compiler is just another program, so strict rules are necessary to make it easier to convert the language into machine language code through procedural programming mechanisms as we're describing here.

Let's take a deeper look at the compilation process for a high-level language like C. Figure 2-2 shows how a compiler breaks down the compilation process in terms of preprocessing, lexical analysis, parsing, building a symbol table, and generating the code.

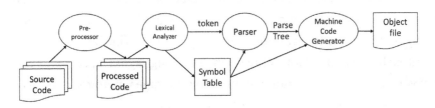

Figure 2-2. *Compilation Process*

The preprocessor looks for specific identifiers in the source code and resolves those to create a file that can be scanned by the next step in the process. In the C language, preprocessor directives start with "#", for example, "#include." The preprocessor will load the file specified by the #include so it becomes part of the source file.

Once the preprocessing is done, the lexical analyzer scans the source file to identify tokens. As it is identifying tokens (e.g., "int" is a keyword, "main" is an identifier, etc.), it updates the symbol table. If there are characters that are not allowed based on the syntax of the program, the lexical analyzer will throw an error. An advanced analyzer may try to recover from the error so it can continue with the compilation process.

The parser does the syntax analysis. It receives the tokens from the lexical analyzer and determines if they are in the appropriate order based on the syntax of the language. Parsers may generate what's called a "parse tree" or an "abstract syntax tree." The parse tree (trees are discussed in Chapter 3) is a representation of the input that conforms to the grammar of the language, and you can generate a version of the original source by walking the tree in the right order. Having a tree-oriented representation of the source code allows the compiler to make multiple passes when generating the machine language without having to reparse the original source. You could also imagine a compiler that creates the parse tree and then uses that to generate multiple output files for different types of processors without having to retokenize and parse the original source code. The parser is also responsible for detecting and reporting syntactical errors (like missing a semicolon), semantic errors (like trying to assign the wrong type of value to a variable), and logical errors (like an infinite loop or unreachable code). Compiling high-level languages is a complex topic, so if you're interested in more detail, we encourage you to read some of the references we've cited at the end of this chapter.

Hopefully you are starting to appreciate why C is considered a high-level language as compared to assembly and machine languages! Since the early 1950s, many high-level programming languages have been created. Fortran, LISP (List Processing), Algol, COBOL (Common Business-Oriented Language), BASIC, Pascal, Smalltalk, SQL (Structured Query Language), Objective-C, C++, Perl, Java, Python, Visual Basic, R, Java, PHP, Ruby, JavaScript, Delphi, C#, Scala, Groovy, Go, PowerShell, and Swift are a few of the more popular languages. Once you understand several of the key programming paradigms, you'll see how many of these languages have quite a bit in common.

Programming Paradigms

So far, we've looked at machine language, assembly language, and C "Hello, World" examples (you may have guessed by now that the first machine language example was a version of "Hello, World"). We recognize that machine language and assembly language are low-level programming languages, and we know how programs are compiled, linked, and loaded. High-level programming languages abstract away the machine language entirely, and the compilation process is broken down into several phases.

Within the classification of high-level programming languages, though, there are several different programming paradigms you should be aware of: imperative, declarative, object-oriented, interpreted, parallel, and machine learning (ML). Learning about these programming paradigms helps you recognize the common elements of many high-level programming languages. Let's take a closer look at each one.

Imperative Programming

Imperative programming is the oldest programming paradigm. Imperative program languages are constructed through a series of well-defined commands in a specific order, and the program flow is controlled by loops and branches. Imperative programs can be broken down into additional programming styles: structured, procedural, and modular.

Structured programming adds sequences, selection, and iteration operations to solve problems with nonstructured imperative programs. Procedural programming is when you divide the program into a small set of procedures, or functions, while modular programming is where you break down the program into a set of modules (files) that can be tested independently of each other.

Imperative programming is typically easier to read and relatively easier to learn because you can easily follow the execution flow, which is why most people learn an imperative programming language first. However, the programs are often much larger, relative to other paradigms, when trying to solve more complex problems. Some alternatives, like functional programming, which is considered a declarative programming paradigm, can do a lot more with less code but are typically harder to learn and read.

Most of the examples we've studied so far have been imperative, so we won't revisit them here. The C programming language is considered an imperative programming language, as well as COBOL, Pascal, Fortran, and many others.

Declarative Programming

With declarative programming, instead of programming based on the steps you go through to arrive at the solution, the program is written by describing the end result. It's also done at a higher level of abstraction. Functional programming is a common type of declarative programming.

In functional programming, the primary rule is that a function has no side effects. It cannot rely on data outside of the function; it can only operate on the data passed to it as parameters. Here's an example of an imperative programming function that violates that rule:

```
int a = 0;

void increment() {
    a = a + 1;
}
```

In this simple example, the increment function takes no arguments, and it is incrementing a variable that is declared outside of the function. This is a valid function in an imperative language like C, but if you're adhering to functional programming rules, you would implement the function this way:

```
int increment( int a ) {
    return a + 1;
}
```

This "increment" example is considered a "pure" function because it only operates on its parameters and thus there can be no side effects like setting the value of a variable outside of the function, and it doesn't keep track of anything between calls. It simply operates on the parameters that are passed to it and nothing else.

Another type of function is one that takes other functions as parameters or returns a function as a result. These are called "higher-order" functions. Consider the following Python code that prints the length of each string in a list. The map function takes a function name as the first parameter and a list of objects (we cover object-oriented programming in the next section) as the second parameter. It simply applies the function to each object in the list and returns the result as a special type of object called an iterator. You then pass the iterator object, which will walk through all of the elements in the data structure, from the map function to a list function to create a list of objects:

```
print( list( map( len, ["programming", "is", "fun"] ) ) )
```

The output looks like this:

```
[11, 2, 3]
```

Here we are able to accomplish the task in one line of code! However, it's not as easy to understand what is going on, is it? The flow of the code isn't obvious because it's about the operations you are performing on the data (in this case, a list of words). To understand it, you read the code from the inside out, so to speak, and also have to understand what the function is going to do, which isn't always obvious.

You have to think differently when writing declarative code, but it can be very powerful. For example, it is easier to execute the operations in parallel. In this case, it's possible to execute the "len" command for each parameter on a different CPU at the same time, which would be very fast!

Writing this code in an imperative way is much different. Let's look at the imperative version, again using Python:

```
word_lengths = [0,0,0]
word_list = ["programming", "is", "fun"]
for i in range(len(word_list)):
    word_lengths[i] = len(word_list[i])
print(list(word_lengths))
```

There are several more lines of code in this example, but it is a little bit easier to follow the flow of execution. However, since the "for" loop operates each command sequentially, it's not as easy for the system to execute the instructions in parallel.

Object-Oriented Programming

Object-oriented programming is an evolution of procedural programming that introduces some very important concepts such as encapsulation, abstraction, inheritance, and polymorphism.

In object-oriented programming, encapsulation is achieved by defining classes of objects. A class defines the private variables that only the methods of that class can act upon, protected variables that only derived classes can access, and public variables the functions and methods outside of the class can access. All of the code that operates on those variables is encapsulated within the class definition. Code external to the class can only use the public mechanisms to interact with an instance of the class. An instance of a class is called an object. For example, in C++, you can define a Vehicle class that has a public method for getting the capacity of the vehicle, but have private and protected properties and methods that are not visible outside of the class:

```cpp
class Vehicle {
  private:
    int access_count = 0;
  protected:
    int capacity = 0;
  public:
    int get_capacity() {
      ++access_count;
      return capacity;
    }
};
```

In this example, the Vehicle has a private variable that increments every time "get_capacity" is executed. However, the capacity variable is set to 0 and is "protected," not "private" like the "access_count" variable. This means classes that derive from the Vehicle class (like a car or bus) can manipulate the capacity variable but not "access_count."

Inheritance is when you define a new "child" class based on the definition of an existing "parent" class. The child class can add additional methods and properties or override the parent implementation and/or add new functionality. We've defined a Vehicle class. Now let's inherit from it to create two new classes, Car and Bus:

```
class Car: public Vehicle {
    public:
        Car() { capacity = 4; }
}

class Bus: public Vehicle {
    public:
        Bus() { capacity = 20; }
}
```

We've introduced a new C++ concept in this example called the "constructor." The constructor has the same name as the class being created. The constructor is called automatically when the object is created. In this example, when you create a Car, it initializes the capacity variable to 4, but when you create a Bus, it initializes the capacity variable to 20. Note that neither class defines the capacity variable because it was defined in the Vehicle parent class. Because the Vehicle class has already specified the function to get the capacity of the vehicle, the child class doesn't have to do anything other than initialize the variable in its constructor. When you create a Bus or Car, you can call those functions that are defined by the Vehicle class, like this:

```
Bus aBus;
int capacity = aBus.get_capacity();
```

We can use the same vehicle example to describe polymorphism, which means having many forms. When you write code that deals with instances of the Vehicle class, you can access the public get_capacity method. It doesn't matter if the object is a bus or car because they both inherit from the Vehicle class. The implementation of get_capacity is different, though, depending on whether or not the object is a car or bus. In this case your code is dealing with vehicles, but they can have different forms. Here's an example where we create a Bus but treat it as a Vehicle:

```
Bus aBus;
Vehicle* aVehicle = &aBus;
int capacity = aVehicle->get_capacity();
```

We declared a variable called "aVehicle" that is a "Vehicle*". That's special syntax in the C language to specify that the "aVehicle" variable is the memory address of another variable that inherits from the Vehicle class. I can "point" that variable at an instance of a Bus object, as in this example, using the "&" operator. The ampersand tells the compiler to use the address of aBus and then assign it to aVehicle. Later, we can change aVehicle to be the address of the Car object. This is how we enable polymorphism in C++. We write our code using the aVehicle variable, and depending on what address it is assigned to, it could be a Car or a Bus.

Now that we've covered the primary concepts common to object-oriented programming languages (encapsulation, inheritance, and polymorphism), we can move on to the interpreted programming paradigm.

Interpreted Programming

Instead of compiling your source code into an executable file, you can use a program called an interpreter and either type in the commands directly at a prompt or put them in a source file and have the interpreter execute it. Interpreters are able to execute the high-level code instructions as they read them instead of compiling and linking into an executable program. The interpreter itself is an executable program that reads the code and interacts with the operating system to do what the code says. Python is the interpreter for the, you guessed it, Python programming language! Let's look at an example of a "hello world" program in Python:

```
print("hello world")
```

Whoa, it's just a single line of code! However, you do have to run this example from the Python program from the command line, which will load and print a prompt (">>>") when it's ready for input, like this:

```
C:\python
Python 3.9.1 (tags/v3.9.1:1e5d33e, Dec  7 2020, 17:08:21) [MSC
v.1927 64 bit (AMD64)] on win32
Type "help", "copyright", "credits" or "license" for more
information.
>>> _
```

Interpreted languages like Python are very powerful. You can easily evaluate code using the interpreter and do rapid testing because you don't have to perform compile/link/load.

JavaScript is another interpreted language that is commonly executed by web browsers like Google Chrome and Microsoft Edge. Instead of running an interpreter from the Windows command line prompt or a Linux terminal, JavaScript is executed by an interpreter in the browser. The script sits on a web server waiting to get downloaded by the browser. In Figure 2-3, the browser requests a page from a web server, which is an HTML document that contains the JavaScript code. JavaScript can be embedded in HTML, or there can be a reference to a JavaScript file in the HTML file. For this example, it's embedded in the HTML file.

Figure 2-3. *Browser Getting a Page from a Web Server*

In Figure 2-4, the browser receives the HTML file containing the JavaScript code from the server. Now the browser has a copy of the script and can start interpreting it.

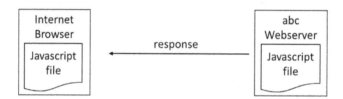

Figure 2-4. *Browser Receiving a Page from a Web Server*

It's very important to understand the context in which your program is executing. For this example, the JavaScript code is executing in the browser, despite its origin being on the server. The script can interact with the browser itself, or it can make calls over the Internet back to the server it was downloaded from to get data or have the server do work on its behalf. This is a very different environment compared to a program that is running entirely on the same machine.

It's also important to realize that interpreted languages can also be imperative, declarative, and object-oriented. Python and JavaScript are both object-oriented and interpreted languages, as well as supporting declarative and imperative mechanisms!

46

Parallel Programming

Parallel programming is when your program takes advantage of multiple CPU cores or Graphics Processing Units (GPUs) to run routines at the same time. A GPU is also a type of processor, but it is designed to run parallel tasks more efficiently. As we saw previously, declarative programming lends itself well to parallel execution. Imperative programming languages add additional mechanisms to help write code that executes in parallel.

First, we should understand how processes work and how they're scheduled by the operating system to run on a CPU. When your program is loaded by the operating system, it's launched as a new process. Your program uses CPU registers and accesses memory as it executes instructions, and there's also the stack that it uses to keep track of function parameters, local variables, and return addresses. If there's just one process running on the system, these resources are used exclusively by that one process, but rarely is that the case. In an operating system like Linux or Windows, there are almost always many more processes loaded into memory than the number of CPU cores that can execute them. Figure 2-5 is a screenshot of the Windows Task Manager's CPU performance screen. On this one machine, there are 225 processes loaded, but only eight cores!

Utilization	Speed		Base speed:	3.60 GHz
10%	4.58 GHz		Sockets:	1
			Cores:	8
Processes	Threads	Handles	Logical processors:	8
224	3392	112844	Virtualization:	Enabled
			L1 cache:	512 KB
Up time			L2 cache:	2.0 MB
5:15:07:25			L3 cache:	12.0 MB

Figure 2-5. *Windows Task Manager CPU Performance Information*

47

The operating system is responsible for scheduling all of these processes on the different cores. In this case, it's possible to run up to eight processes at the same time, one on each core, but we likely need to give CPU time to more than eight processes to keep all aspects of the system running smoothly. The operating system has to use a technique called time slicing to give additional processes CPU time. In short, the operating system initializes the CPU to run a specific process by saving and restoring register values so that the process doesn't need to know it's being time-sliced. The operating system sets a timer on the CPU that will execute the scheduling code when it goes off. Because the operating system is handling this in the background, you don't really need to worry about what the operating system is doing to make this work.

The trick to hide the complexity of process switching from the process itself is memory mapping. With memory mapping, the process thinks it has access to all of physical memory, but in reality, the CPU translates the memory addresses that the process is referencing into physical addresses. Because the program is not using actual physical addresses, the memory that the program references is called "virtual memory." By using virtual memory, the process can assume its stack grows down from the top of memory at the same address every time it executes, but in reality, it is in different pages of physical memory. When the OS switches between processes, it needs to adjust the memory mapping. This is an expensive operation because the CPU has internal buffers that keep track of the mapping so that it happens very quickly. These buffers need to be flushed and get reinitialized when the process switch happens. Thus, a process will suffer a brief performance hit after a process is scheduled to start running.

Threads, on the other hand, are associated with one process and are faster to switch between than processes because the virtual memory map doesn't have to change. Figure 2-6 shows the relationship between a process and its threads.

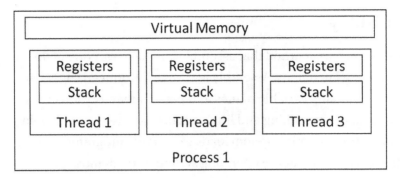

Figure 2-6. *A Process and Its Threads*

When using threads, you need to be very careful since they share resources, memory in particular, with other threads running in the same process. You can run into situations where two threads are trying to change the same memory location and overwrite values in unpredictable ways. To avoid these problems, you have to use techniques like locks and semaphores, discussed later in Chapter 4. You also have to be careful that your threads aren't waiting on each other, in which case they will wait forever, which is called a "deadlock." Writing multi-threaded programs is one of the most difficult programming techniques, but is extremely powerful if you get it right!

Machine Learning

Machine learning is a totally different programing paradigm. Instead of focusing on the flow of the program or writing functions, the computer learns from experience so that it can make predictions in the future. Machine learning is so fundamentally different than other programming paradigms that we decided to devote Chapter 8 to cover it in detail.

Summary

In this chapter, we learned that assembly language was one of the first programming languages. Assembly language introduced some key concepts like using variable names to represent memory locations. A process called compiling and linking is used to create executable programs. The operating system loads executable programs, so they are created in a format that the operating system understands. Operating systems make writing programs much easier by providing services, such as writing to the screen and loading your program into memory. There are many different types of programming techniques you can use to program the computer. We briefly covered imperative, declarative, object-oriented, interpreted and parallel programming.

References and Further Reading

- Alfred V. Aho, Monica S. Lam, Ravi Sethi, and Jeffrey D. Ullman. *Compilers: Principles, Techniques, and Tools*. Pearson Education, Inc. 1986, 2006

- Keith D. Cooper, Linda Torczon. *Engineering a Compiler (Second Edition)*. Morgan Kaufmann, 2011

- John R Levine. *Linkers and Loaders (First Edition)*. Morgan Kaufmann, 1999

- Donald Knuth. *The Art of Computer Programming, Volume 1*. Addison-Wesley, 1968

- Mary Rose Cook. "A practical introduction to functional programming." Publish date not known, retrieved March 2021 <https://maryrosecook.com/blog/post/a-practical-introduction-to-functional-programming>

- Brian Kernighan, Dennis Ritchie. *The* C *Programming Language (Second Edition)*. Pearson, 1988

- Mark Lutz. *Programming Python (Third Edition)*. O'Reilly Media, 2006

CHAPTER 3

Algorithm and Data Structure

Now that we've discussed computer hardware and how to program it to achieve desired purpose, we will discuss how to make programs efficient by leveraging well-known algorithms and data structures for managing logic and data, respectively.

What Is an Algorithm

The dictionary defines an algorithm as a step-by-step procedure for solving a problem or accomplishing some end. In other words, an algorithm is a technique that can be used and communicated to accomplish your goal. Algorithms are not unique to computers. You probably use algorithms every day. The mathematical technique of carrying the one or borrowing from the tens place for addition and subtraction is an algorithm that humans can learn. There is usually more than one algorithm to accomplish your goal. For instance, one algorithm for division is to count the number of times you subtract the divisor from the dividend; this count is the quotient. This is different than finding the largest number the divisor can be multiplied by to be less than the most significant bits of the dividend and then subtracting that value from the dividend to get a new dividend, which is the method most of us learned in school.

© Paul D. Crutcher, Neeraj Kumar Singh, and Peter Tiegs 2021
P. D. Crutcher et al., *Essential Computer Science*,
https://doi.org/10.1007/978-1-4842-7107-0_3

Algorithms can be encoded in any programming language for computers. It should be noted that algorithms for humans are not necessarily optimal for computers to accomplish the same end. This is also true for different computing architectures; an algorithm for a general-purpose CPU will not be the best algorithm for a GPU (Graphics Processing Unit), or quantum computer. In the next section, we will examine how to evaluate algorithms and what trade-offs are made to find the right algorithm for what you need to accomplish.

Good and *Not So Good* Algorithm

Knowing that there are likely multiple algorithms for accomplishing what you want to do, how do we judge what is a good algorithm? What are the factors that we look at? Can we use math to compare algorithms?

One thing that should not be overlooked, but is hard to compare critically, is the readability of a particular algorithm. Most of the software that you write professionally will be viewed and likely maintained by others. Choosing an algorithm that can be read, and more easily maintained, to learn what goal you originally set out to accomplish can be a better choice than the most efficient algorithm. Choosing well-known algorithms can help readability, because there can be plenty of documentation about those algorithms and they can be recognized. Of course, explicitly stating the goal you are seeking to accomplish in source code comments can help.

Time/Space Complexity

One of the main areas where we make trade-offs when selecting or creating algorithms is between the amount of memory, or space, that the algorithm takes and the amount of time it takes to finish.

Asymptotic Notation

Asymptotic notation is a method of writing the complexity of an algorithm in time based on the number of inputs into the algorithm. We cannot simply say that because algorithm 1 will take 7 seconds and algorithm 2 will take 5 seconds, algorithm 2 is better. Asymptotic notation helps by eliminating differences in individual computing machines and programming languages. Taking a closer look at those times, we need to specify the number "n" for the number of items that the algorithm will process to have a realistic measure of its performance to compare against other implementations. For simplicity, let us say n = 100. For algorithm 1, let us say the time it takes to run is 3 + .04n; similarly algorithm 2 takes 0.0005(n^2) seconds to run. As we can see in the graph (Figure 3-1), there is a crossover point in the number of items where algorithm 1 outperforms algorithm 2.

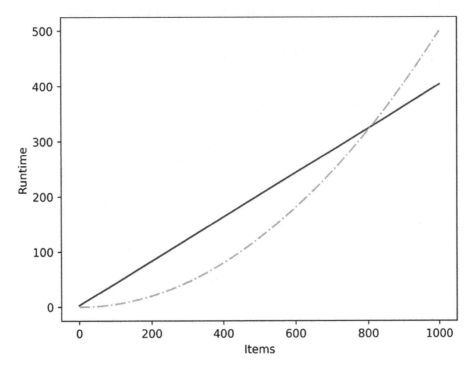

Figure 3-1. *Runtime Comparison Example*

These numbers are on the same computer. If we do analysis on an older computer, we find that algorithm 1 takes 5 + 0.4n or 45 seconds and algorithm 2 takes .005(n^2) or 50 seconds. We will simplify our algorithm by removing constants from the time to allow for differences in computing machines and programming languages. This is called Big-Oh notation as the function for the time an algorithm runs asymptotically approaches the highest degree of the polynomial of n. We will write analysis O(n) for algorithm 1 and O(n^2) for algorithm 2.

With Big-Oh expressions, we generally want to consider "tightness" of the upper bound. While it is correct to say that an algorithm with a time function 3 + 0.4n is O(n), it is a stronger statement to simply say that this algorithm is O(n).

Big-Oh notation is a consistent method for comparing and discussing algorithms across multiple computing machines and programing languages. Table 3-1 is a table of Big-Oh expressions and their informal names.

Table 3-1. *Big-Oh Common Names*

Big-Oh	Name
O(1)	Constant
O(log n)	Logarithmic
O(n)	Linear
O(n log n)	n log n
O(n^2)	Quadratic
O(n^3)	Cubic
O(2^n)	Exponential

Fundamental Data Structures and Algorithms

Now that we have examined what an algorithm is and how we can compare them, we will look at common data structures that hold our data. We will also look at common algorithmic techniques using these data structures.

Store (Data Structure)

There are several structures that can store data. Each of these structures has different advantages, and algorithms may be able to utilize different data structures more efficiently than others.

Stack

A stack is a data structure that reflects the metaphor of a stack of plates. When using a stack, an algorithm operates only on the "top" item in the stack. When that item is operated on, it is removed or "popped" off the stack. A data item may also be "pushed" onto a stack. Because data is only operated on or removed from the "top" of the stack, a stack is sometimes referred to as a FILO (First In, Last Out) or LIFO (Last In, First Out). See Figure 3-2.

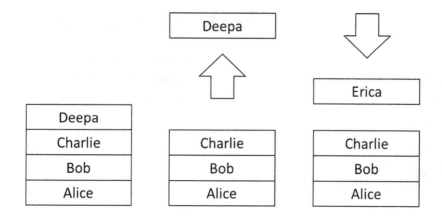

Popped off the Stack   Pushed onto the Stack

Figure 3-2. *Stack Example*

Queue

A queue is another data structure. As you can imagine, a queue also acts like a line to an event. Data items in a queue are added at the "back" of the queue and processed at the "front" of the queue. Queues can vary in length, allowing them to be used as a buffer. Queues are also referred to as FIFOs (First In, First Out). See Figure 3-3.

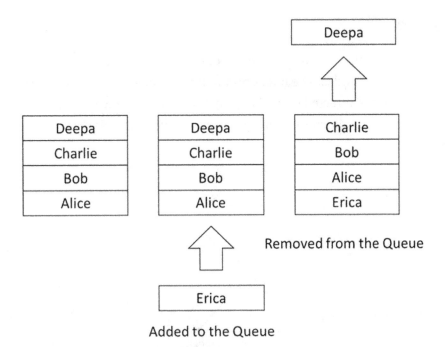

Removed from the Queue

Added to the Queue

Figure 3-3. *Queue Example*

Tree

A tree is another data structure that allows for multiple branches. Data items or nodes are attached to the trunk, which has one or more items attached to it as branches. Each branch can have one or more branches attached to it. Nodes without branches attached to them are referred to as leaf nodes, or simply leaves. See Figure 3-4.

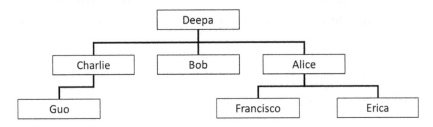

Figure 3-4. *Tree Example*

Graph

A graph is a data structure where nodes or data items are connected via edges to other nodes. The edges may contain data about the relationship to the nodes. A directed graph is a graph data structure where all the edges have a common direction. A tree can be thought of as a directed graph. See Figure 3-5.

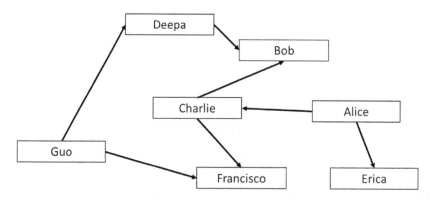

Figure 3-5. *Graph Example*

Linked List

A linked list is another data structure where each node or data item is linked to (connected with one or two) other data items in a chain. A doubly linked list is a list where each node contains a link to both the next node and the previous node. Data items can be inserted into a linked list by connecting to the new data item. Some of the other data structures such as the queue and the stack can be implemented as linked lists. See Figure 3-6.

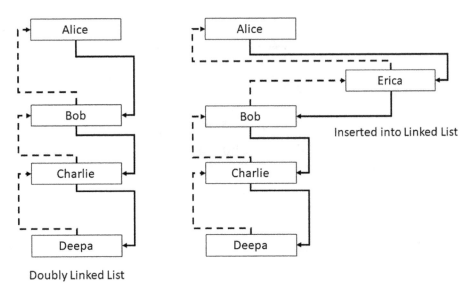

Doubly Linked List

Figure 3-6. *Doubly Linked List Example*

Array

An array is a fixed-size set of data, where each data node is referred to by a coordinate system. In a single-dimensional array, this value is called the index and typically starts at zero for the first node. In a two-dimensional array, or grid, a node has two coordinates like x and y; and in a three-dimensional array, like a cube, it has three, like x, y, and z. Arrays can have more dimensions than three if needed. Data in an array can be accessed from any position in the array at any time. A sparse array is an array that does not have meaningful data in every position. See Figure 3-7.

0	Guo
1	Francisco
2	Erica
3	Deepa
4	Charlie
5	Bob
6	Alice

Figure 3-7. *Array Example*

Dictionary

One more data structure is a dictionary, sometimes referred to as a hash table. Similar to an array, in a dictionary, the data nodes are referred to by a key or index. Unlike an array, this index is not integer values. Instead, a hashing algorithm is run to find a unique value for each data node, and that is used as the key to look up the data node. Like an array, data can be accessed from any node in the hash table at any time. See Figure 3-8.

Guo	f7564f53	Gou Data
Francisco	11773582	Francisco Data
Erica	0826b5c0	Erica Data
Deepa	29987ce1	Deep Data
Charlie	bf779e09	Charlie Data
Bob	9f9d51bc	Bob Data
Alice	6384e2b2	Alice Data

Key	Unique Key Hash Value	Data

Figure 3-8. *Dictionary Example*

Making Use of the Data: Searching, Sorting

Two of the most common things to do with the data in these data structures are to search through the data for a specific item and to sort the data in some fashion. There are different sorting and searching algorithms that can be used on the data. Sorting is often done as part of searching as it can be easier to find an item with the data structure sorted. Depending on the type of data structure, different algorithms will perform better or worse.

The first sorting algorithm that we will look at is the bubble sort (Listing 3-1). In this algorithm, the items are sorted into order with the priority items "bubbling" to the top of the data structure. If we have a linked list, call it I, we will start with the first item (i[0]) in the list and compare it to the next item (i[1]). We then compare i[0] and i[1]; if i[1] is before i[0], then we swap i[0] with i[1]. Then we proceed to compare the new i[1] with i[2]; if i[2] needs to swap with i[1], then we swap. If the items are in the right order, we do not swap but proceed to the next item to compare.

Listing 3-1. Bubble Sort Algorithm in Python

```
1 def bubble(NUMBER_LIST):
2    print(NUMBER_LIST)#Display the unsorted list
3    swap_counter = 0 #Set a counter for the number of swaps 4
5    for idx in range(0, len(NUMBER_LIST)):#Loop through list
6        pos = idx #Set the item to compare
7        swap_pos = pos - 1 #Set the item to swap if needed
8        #Loop through the items to compare
9        while swap_pos >= 0: #Loop through the unsorted list
10           #Check to see if you need to swap
11           if NUMBER_LIST[swap_pos] > NUMBER_LIST[pos]:
12               #Swap positions
13               NUMBER_LIST[pos], NUMBER_LIST[swap_pos] =
                 NUMBER_LIST[swap_pos], NUMBER_LIST[pos]
14               #Increment the swap counter to show the work
15               swap_counter = swap_counter +1
16           print(NUMBER_LIST) # Display the current list
17           #Move to the next swap item
17           swap_pos = swap_pos -1
18           #Move to the next item to compare
19           pos = pos -1
20
21   #Display the number of swaps
22   print("SWAPS:", swap_counter)
```

Python console output
```
>>> bubble.bubble([90,87,82,43,3,5])
[90, 87, 82, 43, 3, 5]
[87, 90, 82, 43, 3, 5]
[87, 82, 90, 43, 3, 5]
[82, 87, 90, 43, 3, 5]
```

```
[82, 87, 43, 90, 3, 5]
[82, 43, 87, 90, 3, 5]
[43, 82, 87, 90, 3, 5]
[43, 82, 87, 3, 90, 5]
[43, 82, 3, 87, 90, 5]
[43, 3, 82, 87, 90, 5]
[3, 43, 82, 87, 90, 5]
[3, 43, 82, 87, 5, 90]
[3, 43, 82, 5, 87, 90]
[3, 43, 5, 82, 87, 90]
[3, 5, 43, 82, 87, 90]
[3, 5, 43, 82, 87, 90]
SWAPS: 14
```

If we do a Big-Oh analysis of this, then we can see this is $O(n^2)$, with the worst case being having to compare every element with every other element.

Selection sort is the next sorting algorithm we will look at (Listing 3-2). In this algorithm, we will compare the first item to the rest of the items and select the smallest item and swap those items. We then proceed with the next item and select the next smallest item and swap them. We proceed until we have iterated through each item in the array. Selection sort is also $O(n^2)$.

Listing 3-2. Selection Sort Algorithm in Python

```
1 def selection(number_list):
2   print(number_list)#Display the unsorted list
3   iter_count = 0 #set a counter for the iterations
4 5   #Loop through the each item on the list
6   for i in range(0, len(number_list)):
7       min_index = i #Set the current min value in the list
8       #Loop through the remaining unsorted list
9       for j in range(i+1, len(number_list)):
```

```
10              #Compare the current item with the current minimum
11              if number_list[j] < number_list[min_index]:
12                  #If the current item is smaller
13                  #make it the new minimum
14                  min_index = j
15              #Swap the new minimum with the
16              #current value in the list
17              number_list[i], number_list[min_index] =
                number_list[min_index], number_list[i]
18              #Increment the count of swaps
19              iter_count = iter_count +1
20          print(number_list): #Display the current list
21      #Display the number of iterations
22      print("Iterations: ", iter_count)
```

Python console output
```
>>> selection.selection([90, 87, 82, 43, 3, 5])
[90, 87, 82, 43, 3, 5]
[5, 90, 87, 82, 43, 3]
[5, 3, 90, 87, 82, 43]
[5, 3, 43, 90, 87, 82]
[5, 3, 43, 82, 90, 87]
[5, 3, 43, 82, 87, 90]
[5, 3, 43, 82, 87, 90]
Iterations:   15
```

Problem Solving Techniques

We have examined how we analyze and compare algorithms. And we have looked at how we can structure our data. Now we will look at common techniques for solving problems.

Recursion

A recursive algorithm is an algorithm where the function calls itself. Recursive functions, or methods, can be very efficient and easy to understand. The following is an example of a very simple recursive algorithm (Listing 3-3) to calculate the Fibonacci sequence. In the Fibonacci sequence, the current value is defined as the sum of the previous two values $F(N) = F(N - 1) + F(N - 2)$. Also the first two values $F(1)$ and $F(0)$ are predefined to 1 and 0, respectively. For example, to calculate the value of $F(3)$, we need to first calculate the $F(2)$ and $F(1)$. To calculate $F(2)$, we need to calculate $F(1)$ and $F(0)$.

$F(1)$ is 1 and $F(0)$ is 0 so that makes $F(2) = 1 + 0$ or 1. To finish calculating $F(3)$, we add $F(2) + F(1)$ or $1 + 1$. Therefore, $F(3)$ is 2.

Listing 3-3. Recursive Fibonacci Algorithm

```
def fibonacci(value):
    if value == 0:#Set F(0) to 0
        retval = value
    elif value == 1:#Set F(1) to 1
        retval = value
    else: #Otherwise calculate the value of F(N)
        #Recursively call the fibonacci function on the
        #previous value. Then call fibonacci function on the
        #value before that.
        #Set the current value to the sum of those two values
        retval = fibonacci(value-1) + fibonacci(value-2)
    return retval

def fibonacci_list(max):
    for i in range(0, max):
        #Display the current Fibonacci value
        print(fibonacci(i))
```

Python console output
```
>>> fibonacci.fibonacci_list(5)
0
1
1
2
3
```

Divide and Conquer

Divide and conquer is a technique where the data is divided and each smaller portion is operated on.

The merge sort algorithm (Listing 3-4) is a good example of both recursion and divide and conquer algorithms. The basic part of the merge sort algorithm splits a list into two separate equal halves. Those halves are then sorted. Once you have two sorted halves, you simply compare the first items in each list and add the smaller to the next position in a new list. To get each half sorted, you can call the merge sort algorithm on each half.

Listing 3-4. Merge Sort Divide and Conquer Algorithm in Python

```
 1 def merge(number_list):
 2    #Check if the list is longer than one element
 3    if len(number_list) > 1:
 4          #Find the middle of the list
 5          half_idx = int(len(number_list)/2)
 6          #Create a list with front half of the list
 7          list_a = number_list[:half_idx]
 8          #Create a list with the back half of the list
 9          list_b = number_list[half_idx:]
10          #Recursively call this merge function
11          #to sort the first half
```

```
12      sorted_a = merge(list_a)
13      #Recursively call this merge function
14      #to sort the second half
15      sorted_b = merge(list_b)
16      #Init an empty list to insert the sorted values
17      sorted_list = []
18      #Set a flag to indicate both lists are inserted
19      done = False
20      while not done: #Iterate on the lists until done
21          #Compare the first item of each list
22          if sorted_a[0] < sorted_b[0]:
23              #When the first list item is smaller
24              # insert into the sorted list
25              sorted_list.append(sorted_a.pop(0))
26          else:
27              #When the second list item is smaller
28              # insert into the sorted list
29              sorted_list.append(sorted_b.pop(0))
30          if len(sorted_a) == 0:
31              #When the first list is empty add the
32              # remainder of the second list to the
33              # sorted list
34              sorted_list = sorted_list + sorted_b
35              #Set the done flag to end the loop
36              done = True
37          elif len(sorted_b) == 0:
38              #When the first list is empty add the
39              # remainder of the second list to the
40              # sorted list
41              sorted_list = sorted_list + sorted_a
42              #Set the done flag to end the loop
```

```
43                    done = True
44           print(sorted_list)
45      else:# If the list is only one element it is sorted
46           sorted_list = number_list
47
48
49    return(sorted_list)
```

Python console output

```
>>> merge.merge([90, 87, 82,43,3,5])
[82, 87]
[82, 87, 90]
[3, 5]
[3, 5, 43]
[3, 5, 43, 82, 87, 90]
[3, 5, 43, 82, 87, 90]
```

Brute Force

A brute force algorithm is just as it sounds, doing the most obvious thing
with the data operating on each data item individually. In some situations,
especially with smaller data sets, this can be the quickest way to solve the
problems, but in general, this is a costly way O()) to perform a function.

Greedy Algorithms

A greedy algorithm is an algorithm that makes a locally optimal decision.
This can, in some cases, lead to locally optimized implementations vs. the
best globally optimized solution. Greedy algorithms include the Huffman
coding algorithm for data compression and the Dijkstra algorithm for
search in a tree.

Class of Problems

Many algorithms can be solved in polynomial time where the Big-Oh expression can be written as a polynomial. These are considered tractable problems. There is also the set of problems that cannot be solved in polynomial time. These are considered intractable. However, within the set of intractable problems are a set of problems that can verify possible answers in polynomial time. These are referred to as nondeterministic polynomial, or NP, problems. Finding a prime number is an example of this type of problem.

NP-Complete and NP-Hard Problems

Within the set of NP problems are the set of problems no one knows how to solve in less than exponential time known as NP-complete.

One common example of an NP-complete problem is the traveling salesman problem, where we want to find the shortest path for a salesman to navigate a set of cities connected by routes of different lengths. Checking the length of a route and comparing it to other routes is polynomial, but finding the shortest route requires going through all possible combinations.

In addition to NP problems are another set of problems that are defined as NP-hard. These problems are as hard as or harder than any NP problems. This set of problems are called NP-hard problems. If these problems are found to be solvable in polynomial time, that would imply that all NP problems are actually solvable in polynomial time. This is not believed to be the case.

Databases

So far in this chapter, we have looked at data structures and algorithms that have been operating on data in system memory (e.g., RAM). Now we will look at database systems that can persistently store and recover the data. A database is simply an organized set of data that is stored apart from the program that will utilize that data.

Persistence and Volume

We separate data out from the software into a database for various reasons. One reason is the persistence of data. If you have software that doesn't, somehow, "save" its resulting data, that data would not be available after the software is run, as it was only in system memory, which will be reused by other programs once your program is done. This storage, or persistence, of data also provides some other advantages. It allows multiple different software applications to access the same data. Many database systems allow for multiple applications to access the data concurrently.

The other reason to store the data separate from the software is that it allows the software to operate on much larger volumes of data than can be contained in the RAM. A database system can provide parts of the data to the software at a time so that software can work on this smaller sets of data.

Fundamental Requirements: ACID

As the volume of data gets larger, and there is more concurrent access (from multiple concurrently running applications) to the data, a database must make sure that it meets the requirements of ACID (Atomicity, Consistency, Isolation, and Durability).

Atomicity means that an update happens to the database as a single, atomic event, so there are no partial updates. Say, for instance, I have a simple database of a name, street address, and zip code. And I need to update a record because someone moved to a new city. A nonatomic update might be to update the zip code without updating the street address, followed by an update of the street address. This would lead to a point in time where the data in the database is incorrect (only partially updated). In contrast, an atomic update, or commit, would update the record with both the new street address and zip code at the same time, so the database is never incorrect.

Consistency means that in the event of a failure, for instance, an update failure, the database stays consistent with a known good state; this is usually the previous state of the database. For example, in our previous example, we may want to update all the names to make sure they are capitalized. If there is a failure after the third record is updated, then the transaction will roll back to the previous state, where none of the names are capitalized.

Isolation means that if there are multiple concurrent updates to the database, each transaction must not be intermixed with any other transaction. The two previous examples for updating one record (a person moved) and updating all the records to make sure that names are capitalized must be isolated. In this case, all the names get updated first, and then the one record is updated with a new street address and zip code. This is important for data consistency and durability. If we needed to roll back a transaction and both sets of changes were intermixed, we would not be able to clearly go back to a known good state.

Durability is like consistency; it means that in the event of a failure of the underlying database system, when the database system restarts, it is able to pick up where it left off and complete the transaction. For example, in the previous example, say that after the third record gets updated, the operating system forces a reboot. When the operating system comes back up, the database system must complete the transaction starting at exactly the fourth record.

Brief History of Database System Evolution

In 1970 Edgar F. Codd wrote a paper describing relational database systems. Prior to the publication of Codd's paper, companies had started to develop database systems based on other models, but by the late 1970s, the relational database model had become prevalent. IBM produced the first prototype relational database with SQL in 1976. The Oracle Database was the first commercial database that implemented the model and featured SQL, the Structured Query Language. Oracle was released in 1977, prior to IBM's release of SQL/DS in 1981, despite IBM having a head start. Also, in 1981, dBase II, considered the first relational database for PCs, was released for personal computers. Oracle became the primary database used in the enterprise as well as the Internet until the release of the open source database MySQL in 1995. On the PC side, many solutions were released over the next decade with Microsoft Access becoming the de facto standard relational database on the PC in 1993.

Most Prominent Current Database Systems

Today, Oracle remains one of the most prominent relational database systems. In addition, the open source community has brought several solutions to prominent usage. MySQL still is in use but is joined by PostgreSQL and SQLite as to the very common open source relational database solutions. On the commercial side, Microsoft SQL Server has also risen to prominence in its usages.

Relational Data and SQL

Relational data is based on set theory and the relationships between sets. Sets can be combined in a union. This means a new set is formed that contains all the data elements that are in the sets combined. A new set, for instance, may be formed from the differences of sets; this would be a set of all of the data elements that are unique between the sets. Furthermore, another set can be formed from the intersection of two sets. This is where a new set is formed from all the elements that are common between the two sets. See Figure 3-9.

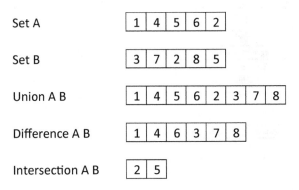

Figure 3-9. *Set Operations Example*

SQL is a standard language to describe these relationships between sets of data to extract meaningful data from a relational database. For example (Figure 3-10), a SQL statement SELECT (id, name, zipcode) FROM people_table WHERE (zipcode IS '97124') forms a set containing the value 97124 and then intersects that data with the set of zip codes in the table. This new intersected set of records will have the same set of fields as the original table but only contain the values for those that match the zip code 97124.

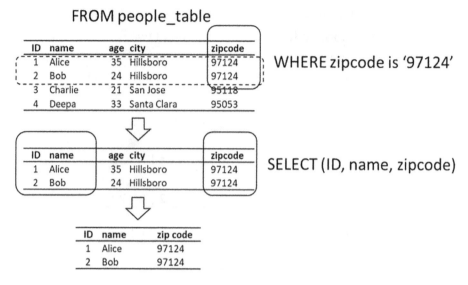

Figure 3-10. *SQL Statement Actions*

SQL syntax allows for a rich group of set relationships described in a machine-translatable language that approximates natural language.

Structured Data/Unstructured Data

Relational databases mostly have structured data, data that is organized into rows and columns. This structured organization makes it easy to interact with the data using SQL and the set relations. The definition of this structure is called a schema. As you can imagine, however, much of the data that we have in the world is not so easily structured. Unstructured data is data that cannot easily be organized into rows and columns, such as natural language text. This rise in unstructured data has also led to an increase in databases that do not follow the same constraints of relational databases.

NoSQL

NoSQL or Not Only SQL is a collective name of a growing set of databases that apply different data structures besides tables of rows and columns used in relational databases.

With the rise of the Internet and service-oriented architectures, one of the key points of integrating the data from multiple applications shifted from the relational database and SQL to service access. This allowed developers to create a closer mapping of the data structures used in the application to the data stored in the database. Now developers could have a much more natural connection between the data that is being stored and the data that is being used.

Examples of NoSQL Databases

We will look at some common examples of NoSQL databases.

Graph DB: Neo4j

Neo4j is a native graph database where the data is stored and its relationship to other data is also stored. A record is stored as a node in a graph data structure, and additional relationship records are stored with information about how various nodes are related (connected) to each other.

Neo4j can be schema-less with nodes having different fields as needed. Neo4j also has its own query language called Cypher.

Column Family DB: Bigtable and Cassandra

Bigtable is a proprietary wide-column family database from Google. Bigtable is designed to specifically handle exceptionally large sets of data.

Like Bigtable, Cassandra is an open source column family database from Apache. A column family database organizes the data into rows and columns. A column is the primary data entity. A column is made up of a name and a value with the name acting as a key in a key-value pair. A row is an arbitrary group of columns with a row key. A column family is a group of rows with some column keys in common. Cassandra is a schema-free database in that rows do not have to have the same columns. Cassandra also has its own query language CQL.

Document DB: CouchDB and MongoDB

CouchDB is a document database from an open source project that is part of the Apache group. Each piece of data is considered a document with its own set of fields.

MongoDB is another open source project that is a document database. It stores records as JSON (JavaScript Object Notation) documents. Each document can have its own set of attributes so it can be schema-free. Both CouchDB and MongoDB have their own mechanisms for querying the data.

Summary

As we have seen throughout this chapter, there are many considerations when working with data. The selection algorithm, data structures, and database for persistent storage should be chosen thoughtfully so that the software can be developed in the most effective way.

References and Further Reading

- Thomas Cormen. *Introduction to Algorithms, Third Edition*. MIT Press, 2009

- Avi Silberschatz. *Database System Concepts*. McGraw-Hill Education, 2010

- Alfred V. Aho and Jeffery D. Ullman. *Foundations of Computer Science*. Computer Science Press, 1992

- Mukesh Negi. *Fundamentals of Database Management System*. BPB Publications, 2019

- Pramod Sadalage and Martin Fowler. *NoSQL Distilled: A Brief Guide to the Emerging World of Polyglot Persistence*. Addison-Wesley Professional, 2013

CHAPTER 4

Operating System

Now that we have discussed the basics of computer hardware and software
fundamentals, we will go over how they work together in this chapter. The
operating system abstracts interaction to the HW and makes it efficient
and convenient for software to leverage those HW resources.

When a computer turns on, the processor will execute the instructions
that are presented to it; generally, the first code that runs is for the boot
flow. For a computer that is used for general purposes and after it has
booted up, there may be a variety of applications that need to be run on
it simultaneously. Additionally, there could be a wide range of devices
that could be connected to the computer (not part of the main system,
for instance). All these need to be abstracted and handled efficiently and
seamlessly. The user expects the system to "just work." The operating
system facilitates all of this and more.

What Is an Operating System

An operating system, commonly referred to as the OS, is a program that
controls the execution of other programs running on the system. It acts
as a facilitator and intermediate layer between the different software
components and the computer hardware as shown in Figure 4-1.

© Paul D. Crutcher, Neeraj Kumar Singh, and Peter Tiegs 2021
P. D. Crutcher et al., *Essential Computer Science*,
https://doi.org/10.1007/978-1-4842-7107-0_4

When any operating system is built, it focuses on three main objectives:

- Efficiency of the OS in terms of responsiveness, fluidity, and so on

- Ease of usability to the user in terms of making it convenient

- Ability to abstract and extend to new devices and software

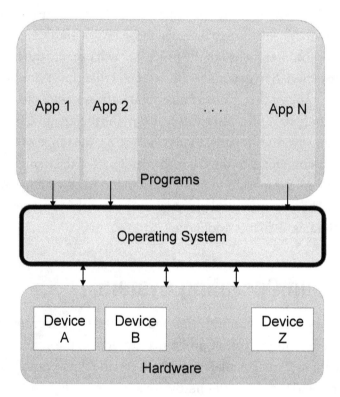

Figure 4-1. *High-Level Overview of an Operating System*

Let us take a quick look at how this is implemented. Most OSs typically have at least two main pieces:

- There is a core part that handles the complex, low-level functionalities and is typically referred to as the kernel.

- There are generally some libraries, applications, and tools that are shipped with the OS. For example, there could be browsers, custom features, frameworks, and OS-native applications that are bundled together.

Although the latter are generally referred to be a part of the OS, for the rest of our discussion, we will be focusing on the OS kernel.

Few common examples of operating systems that are prevalent are listed below. This list is not meant to be comprehensive but give the user a high-level idea of the list of operating systems that are commonly prevalent:

- Microsoft Windows

- GNU/Linux-based OS

- macOS (used for Apple's computers and client models)

- iOS (used for Apple's smartphone/tablet models)

- Android

All of these operating systems have different generations, versions, and upgrades. Some of the features supported across OS builds may also vary from time to time. However, in general, the core concepts discussed in this chapter are applicable to all of them.

OS Categories

The OSs can be categorized based on the different methods in use. The two most common methodologies are by the **usage type** and the **design/supported features** of the OS.

The first methodology is based on how the system is used. Based on this, there are five main categories:

1. Batch: For usages where a sequence of steps needs to be executed repeatedly without any human intervention. These classes are called batch OSs.

2. Time Sharing: For systems where many users access common hardware, there could be a need to time-share the limited resources. The OSs in such cases are categorized as time-sharing OSs.

3. Distributed: For hardware that is distributed physically and a single OS needs to coordinate their access, we call these systems distributed OSs.

4. Network: Another usage model, similar to the distributed scenario, is when the systems are connected over an IP (Internet Protocol) network and therefore referred to as network OSs.

5. Real Time: In some cases, we need fine-grained time precision in execution and responsiveness. We call these systems real-time OSs.

The second methodology is based on the **design and supported features** of the operating system. Based on this, there are three main categories:

1. Monolithic: In this case, the entire OS is running in a high-privilege kernel space and acts as the supervisor for all other programs to run. Common monolithic OSs include many of the UNIX flavors.

2. Modular: In some OSs, a few parts of the OS are
    implemented as so-called plug-and-play modules
    that can be updated independent of the OS kernel.
    Many modern OSs follow this methodology, such as
    Microsoft Windows, Linux flavors, and macOS.

3. Microservice based: More modern OSs are emerging
    and leverage the concept of microservices where
    many of the previously monolithic OS features
    may be broken down into smaller parts that run in
    either the kernel or user mode. The microservice
    approach helps in assigning the right responsibility
    of the components and easier error tracking and
    maintenance. Some versions of Red Hat OS support
    microservices natively.

Why We Need an OS

As we discussed before, the OS needs to be able to facilitate different
applications running on the system. For example, consider an application
that wants to play music from the file system and another application
that needs to create a file and write to the disk. In both these cases, these
applications need to access storage, must be able to render/display some
content on the screen, and may need to access additional devices on the
system.

Let us consider two very different approaches to enabling the
preceding example. One approach could be that each of the applications
will run directly on the HW with no OS abstraction; in this case, they must
each implement all of the required functionality including hardware access
and resource management on their own. This approach has some obvious
challenges. One problem is the size of the resultant programs; they must
have code for their application logic as well as all of the lower-level code

for accessing hardware. This will increase the number of defects in the code and increase the time it takes to get the application working correctly. Another problem is that the application may not be able to handle all types of hardware and devices. For example, the application would need to encode specific functions to support a given storage device, but another storage device on a slightly different system may be different enough that the application will fail there. Also, with this approach, you would not be able to run the two applications at the same time; they would need to run sequentially, since there is no mechanism to allow two programs to run at the same time in this scenario. Another, more mainstream approach would be for a common program to facilitate all the interactions with the hardware, handle complexities that happen underneath, and provide an abstraction for the applications to interact to. This allows the applications to focus on their business logic, reducing the size and complexity of the resultant application, which also gets the application written and validated much faster.

Before we can decide which is a better approach, let us take a similar analogy with a building construction company that is developing a new gated community. As part of the community, there could be many houses that need to be built. For each of these houses, there could be several common requirements such as water piping, electricity lines, drainage system, and so on that may be needed. Each of the individual houses may handle these on its own and have its own separate blueprints for water, drainage, communication, and so on. But it doesn't scale. With this example, we can see that this is inefficient and often messy in terms of provisioning the lines and piping as well as supporting and maintaining them, in the long term. The best practice here is for the engineering team to streamline these via a central pipeline and then branch off from the central line to the individual houses as per the requirements. This not only saves cost, it is easier to maintain and manage and is less error-prone. The same concept can be applied for the case of a computing device, where the OS manages and streamlines usage of hardware resources and allows multiple applications to run in parallel with each other.

In practice, there are many common features that may be needed by your programs including, for example, security, which would have services like encryption, authentication, and authorization, to name a few. It makes sense for these kinds of capabilities to be provided by the operating system, so they can be leveraged consistently by all.

Purpose of an OS

As a precursor to this section, consider a common home appliance such as a dishwasher. The appliance supports a set of functionalities that is usually predefined (more modern systems may additionally have some programmability) in manufacturing. Such modern appliances have microprocessors with their runtime code already loaded and configured so that they "know" exactly what to do. Here, the complete programming logic is embedded into a non-volatile memory that is later executed using a microcontroller. It still has complexities in terms of reliability, error handling, and timing. However, the environment and the variabilities are quite contained within the appliance.

In the case of a general-purpose computing device, as we discussed earlier, there are varying needs in terms of the underlying hardware, the applications that need to run on the system, and the support for different users. At a high level, many of these are not deterministic in nature and could vary from one system to another. The purpose of the operating system is to ensure that it abstracts the HW and facilitates the seamless execution of our applications using the system. Now, we will take a more detailed look at the different complexities on such systems and how the OS handles them.

Complex and Multiprocessor Systems

Many modern computing architectures support microprocessors with multiple CPU cores. On higher-end systems, there could even be multiple sockets each able to host a microprocessor (with several cores). Typically, when all cores provide the same or identical capabilities, they are called as homogeneous platforms. There could also be systems that provide different capabilities on different CPU cores. These are called heterogeneous platforms. There are also additional execution engines such as Graphics Processing Units (GPUs), which accelerate graphics and 3D processing and display, for instance. An operating system supporting such a platform will need to ensure efficient scheduling of the different programs on the different execution engines (cores) available on the system. Similarly, there could be differences in the hardware devices on the platform and their capabilities such as the type of display used, peripherals connected, storage/memory used, sensors available, and so on. It may not be possible to release a new OS for every new system configuration. Hence, the OS would also be required to abstract the differences in the hardware configurations to the applications.

Multitasking and Multifunction Software

There is also an increasing need to use computers for multiple tasks in parallel. Let's build on the same example that we had before where a user may want to play music and also create a content and write a file at the same time. In general, there could be many such applications that may need to be running on the system at the same time. These could include applications that the user initiated, so-called "foreground" applications, and applications that the OS has initiated in the background for the effective functionality of the system. It is the OS that ensures the streamlined execution of these applications.

Multiuser Systems

Often, there could be more than one user of a system such as an administrator and multiple other users with different levels of access permission who may want to utilize the system. It is important to streamline execution for each of these users so that they do not find any perceived delay of their requests. At the same time, there need to be controls in place to manage privacy and security between users. The OS facilitates and manages these capabilities as well.

As we discussed earlier, in general, there are various dynamic scenarios on the platform, and it is the role of the operating system to handle these in a consistent, safe, and performant manner. Most general-purpose OSs in use today, such as Windows, Linux, macOS, and so on, provide and handle most of the preceding complexities. Figure 4-2 shows a slightly detailed view of an abstract operating system.

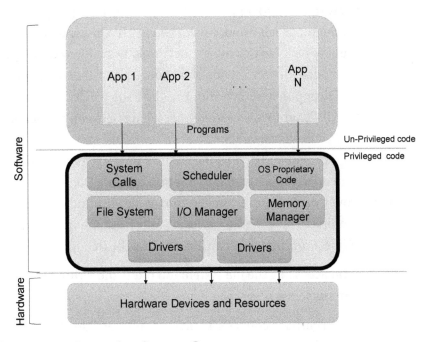

Figure 4-2. Operating System Components

As we can see here, it supports multiple different hardware, supports co-existence of multiple applications, and abstracts the complexities. The OS exposes different levels of abstractions for applications and drivers to work together. Typically, there are APIs (application programming interfaces) that are exposed to access system resources. These APIs are then used by programs to request for communicating to the hardware. While the communication happens, there could be requests from multiple programs and users at the same time. The OS streamlines these requests using efficient scheduling algorithms and through management of I/Os and handling conflicts.

Why Is It Important to Know About the OS?

Software developers must have a good understanding of the environment, the OS, that their code is running in, or they won't be able to achieve the things they want with their program. As you, a software developer, go through the stages of development, it is important for you to keep in mind the OS interfaces and functionality as this will impact the software being developed.

For a given application, the choice of language and needed runtime features may be OS dependent. For example, the choice of inter-process communication (IPC) protocols used for messaging between applications will depend on the OS offerings.

During development and debug, there could be usages where the developer may need to understand and interact with the OS. For example, debugging a slowly performing or nonresponsive application may require some understanding of how the OS performs input/output operations. Here are some questions that may come up during the debug:

- Are you accessing the file system too often and writing repeatedly to the disk?

- Is there a garbage collector in place by the software framework/SDK?

- Is the application holding physical memory information for too long?

- Is the application frequently creating and swapping pages in memory? What it the average commit size and page swap rate?

- Is there any other system event such as power event, upgrades, or virus scanning that could have affected performance?

- Is there an impact on the application based on the scheduling policy, application priority, and utilization levels?

If the application needs to interface with a custom device, it will most likely need to interface some low-level functionality provided by the OS. For example, if there was a custom device that is connected to the system, the application would need to use the OS-provided API for communication. As a software developer, it may be required to understand these APIs and leverage the OS capabilities. There could also be a need to follow certain standard protocols provided by the OS for authenticating a given user of your application to grant permissions and access.

The list can grow based the variety of applications and their intended usages. As we discussed before, the design considerations for the OS must leverage appropriate abstraction and separation of concerns between different hardware and users. Also, most OSs are tuned and optimized for some common use cases, based on expected use. From a software developer point of view, it is important to be aware of some of these and leverage the configuration knobs and built-in tools provided by the OS.

Responsibilities of an OS

As we have seen in the previous sections, the OS needs to be able to abstract the complexities of the underlying hardware, support multiple users, and facilitate execution of multiple applications at the same time. In Table 4-1, we articulate some of these requirements and discuss how an OS can achieve them.

Table 4-1. *Requirements and Solutions*

Requirement	Solution
Applications require time on the **CPU** to execute their instructions.	The OS shall implement and abstract this using suitable **scheduling** algorithms.
Applications require access to system **memory** for variable storage and to perform calculations based on values in memory.	The OS shall implement **memory management** and provide APIs for applications to utilize this memory.
Each software may need to access different **devices** on the platform.	The OS may provide APIs for **device and I/O management** and interfaces through which these devices can be communicated.
There may be a need for the user or applications to save and read back contents from the **storage**.	Most OSs have a **directory and file system** that handles the storage and retrieval of contents on the disk.
It is important to perform all of the core operations listed in the preceding **securely** and efficiently.	Most OSs have a **security subsystem** that meets specific security requirements, virtualizations, and controls and balances.
Ease of access and usability of the system.	The OS may also have an additional GUI (graphical user interface) in place to make it easy to use, access, and work with the system.

To summarize, the OS performs different functions and handles multiple responsibilities for software to co-exist, streamlining access to resources, and enabling users to perform actions. They are broadly classified into the following functional areas:

- **Scheduling**

- **Memory management**

- **I/O and resource management**

- **Access and protection**

- **File systems**

- **User interface/shell**

The remainder of this part of this chapter will look at the preceding areas one by one.

Scheduling

One of the primary functionalities of the OS would be to provide the ability to run multiple, concurrent applications on the system and efficiently manage their access to system resources. As many programs try to run in parallel, there may be competing and conflicting requests to access hardware resources such as CPU, memory, and other devices. The operating system streamlines these requests and orchestrates the execution at runtime by scheduling the execution and subsequent requests to avoid conflicts.

Before we go into the details of scheduling responsibilities and algorithms, it is important to know some background about the basic concepts of program execution, specifically processes and threads.

Program and Process Basics

When a software developer builds a solution, the set of capabilities it provides is usually static and embedded in the form of processed code that is built for the OS. This is typically referred to as the program. When the program gets triggered to run, the OS assigns a process ID and other metrics for tracking. At the highest level, an executing program is tracked as a process in the OS. Note that in the context of different operating systems, jobs and processes may be used interchangeably. However, they refer to a program in execution.

Process States

When a program gets triggered for execution, typically say using a double click of the EXE (or using a CreateProcess() API in Windows), a new process is created. A process typically supports multiple states of readiness in its lifecycle. The following diagram captures some generic process execution states.

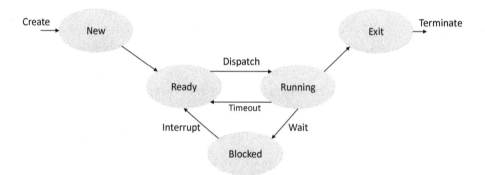

Figure 4-3. *Process States and Transitions*

As we can see in Figure 4-3, the process begins "life" in the **New** state just after it is created. From there it may move to other states, with the next state typically being the **Ready** state, where it is waiting for the

OS to assign a CPU to run on. The OS has a scheduler that takes care of selecting a process from a list of processes to be executed. Once selected, the dispatcher comes in that ensures the process selected gets time on the CPU. At this point, the process moves to the **Running** state. There could be a case when a process is running on the CPU, but may not have completed its job. The OS would also have to ensure other processes on the system get a fair share of time on the CPU. So the OS continues to execute the process on the CPU till a "timeout" is reached. After which, the process could be moved back to the Ready state waiting to be dispatched. This sequence of steps can continue to happen. At a later point, if the process is waiting on a device I/O, say a disk, it could be moved to the **Blocked** state if the device is busy. The same process continues till the process gets terminated and moves to the **Exit** state.

Note that there could be more than one CPU core on the system and hence the OS could schedule on any of the available cores. In order to avoid switching of context between CPU cores every time, the OS tries to limit such frequent transitions. The OS monitors and manages the transition of these states seamlessly and maintains the states of all such processes running on the system.

Process Control Block (PCB)

The OS has a well-defined data structure through which it manages different processes and their states. It is called as the Process Control Block (PCB). As we can see in Figure 4-4, the PCB includes all information that is required to manage and monitor the process. It includes details such as the unique identifier of the process, current state, and other details pertaining to accounting and scheduling. It may also store the processor register details, program counter (which contains the address of the next instruction to be executed), and memory information. All these are required to execute the process and also save the context of the process when it is moved from one state to the other as we discussed previously.

Figure 4-4. *Process Control Block (PCB) Representation*

- The **process ID** is a unique identifier for the instance of the process that is to be created or currently running.

- The **process state** determines the current state of the process, described in the preceding section.

- The **pointer** could refer to the hierarchy of processes (e.g., if there was a parent process that triggered this process).

- The **priority** refers to the priority level (e.g., high, medium, low, critical, real time, etc.) that the OS may need to use to determine the scheduling.

- **Affinity and CPU register details** include if there is a need to run a process on a specific core. It may also hold other register and memory details that are needed to execute the process.

- The **program counter** usually refers to the next instruction that needs to be run.

- **I/O and accounting** information such as paging requirements, devices assigned, limits, and so on that is used to monitor each process is also included in the structure.

There could be some modifications to how the PCB looks on different OSs. However, most of the preceding are commonly represented in the PCB.

Now that we have looked at how a process is represented in the OS and how the OS maintains the context of different processes, we will look at how the OS supports multitasking and how these processes are scheduled.

Context Switching

The operating system may need to swap the currently executing process with another process to allow other applications to run, if the current process is running for too long (preventing other processes/applications from running). It does so with the help of context switching.

When a process is executing on the CPU, the process context is determined by the program counter (instruction currently run), the processor status, register states, and various other metrics. When the OS needs to swap a currently executing process with another process, it must do the following steps:

1. Pause the currently executing process and save the context.

2. Switch to the new process.

3. When starting a new process, the OS must set the context appropriately for that process.

This ensures that the process executes exactly from where it was swapped. With CPUs running at GHz frequencies, this is typically not perceivable to the user. There are other hardware interfaces and support to optimize these. For example, the time taken to save and restore context could be automatically supported in certain hardware, which could improve the performance further.

Scheduling

The most frequent process states are the Ready, Waiting, and Running states. The operating system will receive requests to run multiple processes at the same time and may need to streamline the execution. It uses process scheduling queues to perform this:

1. Ready Queue: When a new process is created, it transitions from New to the Ready state. It enters this queue indicating that it is ready to be scheduled.

2. Waiting Queue: When a process gets blocked by a dependent I/O or device or needs to be suspended temporarily, it moves to the Blocked state since it is waiting for a resource. At this point, the OS pushes such process to the Waiting queue.

3. In addition, there could be a **Job queue** that maintains all the processes in the system at any point in time. This is usually needed for bookkeeping purposes.

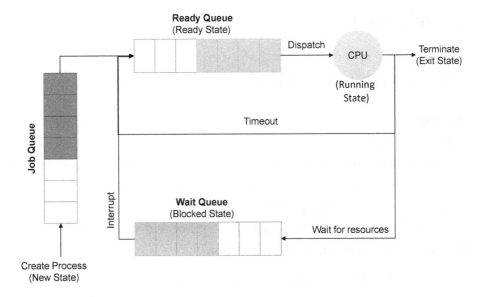

Figure 4-5. *Scheduling Flow in a Typical OS with Different Process States*

As we can see in Figure 4-5, all processes go through the Job queue and are waiting to be dispatched for execution. Once they are assigned CPU time, they get scheduled to run on the CPU for a specific time period. This is called as the quanta of time for which the process gets to run on the CPU. Once that time period is elapsed, the process is moved back to the Ready queue, where it waits to be scheduled again, until it has completed its task. If the process is running and gets blocked waiting on some I/O or an external event, the OS moves the process to the Waiting queue so that it is not wasting time on the CPU. This process of Ready -> Schedule -> Wait continues till the process completes its task, at which time it moves to the Exit state and gets released.

Typically, any process can be compute or I/O intensive depending on what kind of problem it is trying to solve. As a software developer, it is important for you to balance these requirements and optimize the code, perhaps utilizing threads, locks, and critical sections appropriately for best behaviors.

Scheduling Criteria

Most operating systems have predefined criteria that determine the scheduling priorities. Some of them have a criterion to provide maximum throughput and utilization of the CPU effectively, while others may have a higher preference to minimize the turnaround time for any request that comes to the scheduler. Often, most general-purpose operating systems provide a balance between the two and are usually tuned to the general workload needs. There may be additional power and performance settings that can be tuned to modify these behaviors.

Some of the typical metrics that the OS may use to determine scheduling priorities are listed in the following:

- CPU Utilization and Execution Runtime: The total amount of time the process is making use of the CPU excluding NOP (no-operation) idle cycles.

- Volume/Execution Throughput: Some OSs may need to support certain execution rates for a given duration.

- Responsiveness: The time taken for completion of a process and the average time spent in different queues.

- Resource Waiting Time: The average time taken on external I/Os on the system.

Based on these criteria and the strategic needs for the OS, the scheduling behavior of the system is defined.

Note   Most OSs try to ensure there is fairness and liveness in scheduling. There are various scheduling algorithms like First Come, First Serve (FCFS), Shortest Job First (SJF), Shortest Remaining Time First (SRTF), Round-Robin, Static/Dynamic Priority, and so on that the OS uses for scheduling of processes.

Thread Concepts

Now that we have looked at how the process works and how the OS manages the scheduling of a process, we will look at an interesting concept called threads. A thread is nothing more than a lightweight process. When a process gets executed, it could create one or more threads internally that can be executed on the processor. These threads have their own program counter, context, and register information, similar to how the process is managed.

Threads help in performing parallelism within the same process. For example, if we have a simple form application that is executed, it typically starts with a main thread on which the user interface is running. Let's assume we need to read some content that may take a while to load. This could cause the main thread to be blocked preventing the user from interacting with the application. However, if the call is made asynchronously, on another thread, the main thread can continue to run while the content read is happening. This not only improves performance, it also enhances the user experience. Note that all of this happens within the context of the same process.

Let us consider an example of a process that contains a single thread vs. the same process with multiple threads. As we can see in Figure 4-6, the parallel execution across threads happens within the context of the same process. Even if one thread in a process may be blocked, the other thread could continue its execution. Overall, this helps in completing the job faster. Since threads run within the context of a process, they relatively consume lesser system resources than processes as well.

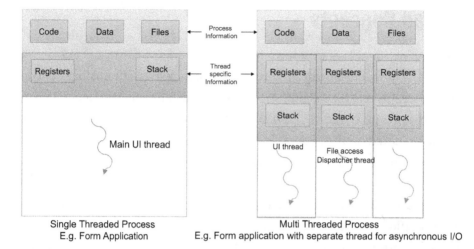

Figure 4-6. *Single- vs. Multi-threaded Process for a Simple Form Application*

The OS may employ different types of threads, depending on whether they are run from an application. For instance, an application may leverage **user-mode threads**, and a kernel driver may leverage **kernel-mode threads**. The OS also handles switching from user-mode threads to kernel-mode threads as required by a process.

Memory Management

In systems with multiple programs running in parallel, there could be many processes in memory at the same time, and each process may have specific memory needs. Processes may need memory for various reasons. First, the executable itself may need to be loaded into memory for execution. This is usually the instructions or the code that needs to be run. The second item would be the data part of the executable. These could be hardcoded strings, text, and variables that are referenced by the process. The third type of memory requirement could arise from runtime requests for memory. These could be needed from the stack/heap for the program to perform its execution.

Further, the operating system may also have its memory requirements. The OS and the kernel components may also need to be loaded in memory. Additionally, there may be a specific portion of memory needed for specific devices. For example, memory-mapped (discussed later) data for a specific device may need to be carved out and handled separately.

Like many other resources, the OS also needs to ensure efficient usage of memory. This is usually handled by the memory management subsystem. It manages various functions including allocation of new memory requests, translation of physical to virtual memories, swapping data pages, protection of specific memory pages, and so on. It may also need to manage and abstract the underlying hardware differences including memory controller intricacies and memory layout specifics. We will cover some of these topics in this section. Before we can get into the details, let's cover some basic concepts.

Address Binding

Consider a short line of pseudo-code (A = B + 2) that adds 2 to variable "B" and assigns this to variable "A". When this line gets compiled, it gets translated into a few steps. The first step would be to read the value of B from memory. The next step would be a simple mathematical calculation to add value 2 to B and perhaps store this in the accumulator. The final step would be to copy back this value and write this back to the memory location referenced by A. As we can see here, there are multiple references to read from memory and write back to memory, also, not shown here, involving the CPU registers. If these A and B are fixed memory locations like in the case of a traditional embedded system, these locations may not change. However, in the case of a general-purpose operating system, it becomes difficult to assign a location in memory that is static from run to run or even for the duration of one run.

To solve this problem, the common solution is to map the program's compiled addresses to the actual address in physical memory. In the simplest case, each program would get its own physical memory. This ensures that multiple programs can co-exist at the same time. This address binding can be done in multiple ways:

1. The address locations could be fixed at compile time. That is, the base address or the starting address of a program can be fixed while compiling, and the rest of the locations are referenced from that. This is not advisable since the fixed base address may not be available if another program is using it or may call for unexpected security violations.

2. The relative address of the program could be calculated at the time the program is loaded. A typical usage model would be to calculate this at runtime using a translation layer, which maps the program address to the real physical address. This is typically handled by the memory controller and is usually the most flexible option. Most operating systems and compilers also default to this mode for security reasons to change the base address at every launch.

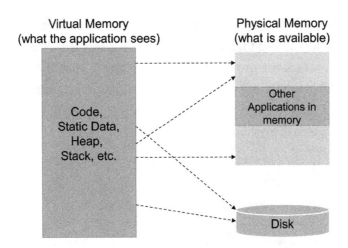

Figure 4-7. *Virtual Memory to Physical Memory Overview*

The address that the program has access to is usually referred to as the virtual address, and the actual location in memory is the physical address on the system. This could refer to a physical location on the RAM. As we can see in Figure 4-7, the application sees its code, static data, the variables, the stack, and so on. However, internally, the memory controller and the OS translate these to a location in physical memory. Not everything that the application sees may be residing in physical memory all the time. Also, at times, certain parts of the data could also be retrieved from storage such as disks. In the next section, we will look at how a simple translation happens between virtual memory and physical memory.

Logical vs. Physical Address

A program will have variables, instructions, and references that are included as part of the source code. The references to these are usually referred to as the symbolic addresses. When the same program gets compiled, the compiler translates these addresses into relative addresses.

This is important for the OS to then load the program in memory with a given base address and then use the relative address from that base to refer to different parts of the program. At this time, the OS can make use of the physical address mapping to refer to specific locations in memory. This is depicted in Figure 4-8 where the relative address is calculated using the base address and the offset.

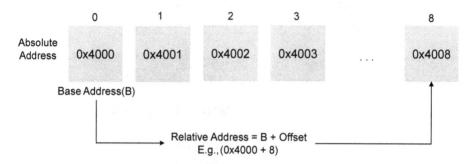

Figure 4-8. *Absolute, Base, and Relative Address Concepts*

In general, there is not enough physical memory to host all programs at the same time. This leads to the concept of virtual memory that can be mapped to physical memory. The memory management unit is responsible for translating virtual addresses to physical addresses. Typically, most OSs have a page table, which is like a lookup table, that is used to translate virtual addresses to a physical address at runtime. When the contents that need to be referred are outside the page, the memory content is then swapped to the new page at runtime. As shown in Figure 4-9, an unwanted page is usually identified and moved out to the secondary disk. Then, the required page is moved into memory to continue with the execution.

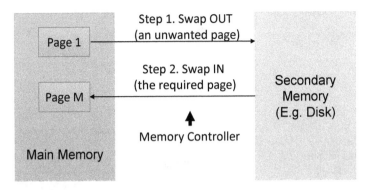

Figure 4-9. *Page Swapping Example*

Inter-process Communication

It is often desirable to have processes communicate with each other to coordinate work, for instance. In such cases, the OS provides one or more mechanisms to enable such process-to-process communication. These mechanisms are broadly classified as inter-process communication (IPC). There are many ways IPCs can be implemented. The two common ways are explained in the following, which involve shared memory and message passing.

Shared Memory Method

When two or more processes need to communicate with each other, they may create a shared memory area that is accessible by both processes. Then, one of the processes may act as the producer of data, while the other could act as the consumer of data. The memory acts as the communication buffer between these two processes. This is a very common mechanism to communicate between processes. This is depicted in Figure 4-10.

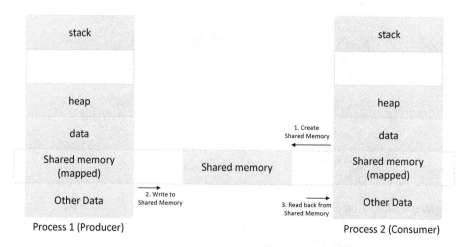

Figure 4-10. *Simple Shared Memory–Based Inter-process Communication*

There are additional details on the timing, creation of memory itself, permissions, and so on. However, we will not cover the details in this book.

Message Passing Method

The other method is called message passing where the two processes have a predefined communication link that could be a file system, socket, named pipe, and so on and a protocol-based messaging mechanism that they use to communicate.

Typically, the first step would be to establish the communication channel itself. For example, in the case of a TCP/IP communication, one of the processes could act as the server waiting on a specific port. The other process could register as a client and connect to that port. The next step could involve sharing of messages between the client and server using predefined protocols leveraging Send and Receive commands. The processes must agree on the communication parameters and flow for this to be successful. Given this, they can communicate until the IPC is terminated by either of the process. This is a common communication mechanism that is used by networking applications as well.

Further Reading

The memory management unit forms a critical part of the operating system. Additionally, some OSs use Translation Lookaside Buffers (TLBs), which contain page entries that have been recently used, multilevel page tables, and page replacement algorithms to perform optimal memory management depending on the needs. The performance, thrashing of memory, and segmentation needs vary from one OS to another. Some of these concepts are covered by the references shared later in this chapter.

I/O Management

As part of the system, there could be multiple devices that are connected and perform different input-output functions. These I/O devices could be used for human interaction such as display panel, touch panels, keyboard, mouse, and track pads, to name a few. Another form of I/O devices could be to connect the system to storage devices, sensors, and so on. There could also be I/O devices for networking needs that implement certain parts of the networking stack. These could be Wi-Fi, Ethernet, and Bluetooth devices and so on.

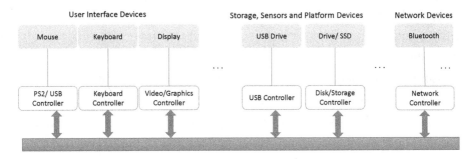

Figure 4-11. *Example I/O Controllers on a System*

As we can see in Figure 4-11, there are varied sets of I/O devices, and each of them has a specific purpose and programming interface. They vary from one to another in the form of protocols they use to communicate such as the data format, speed at which they operate, error reporting mechanisms, and many more. However, from an abstraction point of view, the OS presents a unified I/O system that abstracts the complexity from applications. The OS handles this by establishing protocols and interfaces with each I/O controller. However, the I/O subsystem usually forms the complex part of the operating system due to the dynamics and the wide variety of I/Os involved.

I/O Subsystem

Input/output devices that are connected to the computer are called peripheral devices. There could be additional lines that are used to connect to these devices for communication purposes. These are called buses that are a combination of "data lines" to transfer data, "control lines" to control a device, and "address lines" that may be used to specify address locations. There could be different buses or device protocols that an operating system may support. The most common protocols include Peripheral Component Interconnect Express (PCIe) protocol, Inter-Integrated Circuit (I2C), Advanced Configuration and Power Interface (ACPI), and so on. A device can be connected over one or more of these interfaces.

Consider the need to send a request to read the temperature of a specific device that is connected via ACPI. In this case, the operating system sends a request to the ACPI subsystem, targeting the device that handles the request and returns the data. This is then passed back to the application. In another example, we want to change the display brightness of the display device. In this case, a request is made from the application to the OS, which in turn detects the display device from the I/O subsystem and requests the appropriate display brightness control setting. The display subsystem then makes the necessary action and returns the result, for example, success or failure, back to the OS. All of these happen in a seamless fashion so that the user is not aware of the intricacies involved. Typically, there is a software component in kernel mode called as the "device driver" that handles all interfaces with a device. It helps with communicating between the device and the OS and abstracts the device specifics. Similarly, there could be a driver at the bus level usually referred to as the bus driver. Most OSs include an inbox driver that implements the bus driver. As we saw in Figure 4-11, there is usually a driver for each controller and each device.

The I/O devices can be broadly divided into two categories called block and character devices. Usually, most devices would have a command and data location and a protocol that the device firmware and the driver understand. The driver would fill the required data and issue a command. The device firmware would respond back to the command and return an error code that is utilized by the driver. The protocol, size, and format could differ from one device to another.

Block Devices

These are devices with which the I/O device controller communicates by sending blocks of data. A block is referred to as a group of bytes that are referred together for Read/Write purposes. For example, when a request is made to write a file to the storage disk or if we need to transfer a file to a connected USB drive or if we need to read an image from a connected camera, the transfers are made as block reads. These could be defined by the device, for example, in multiple blocks of 512 or 1024 bytes. The device driver would access by specifying the size of Read/Writes.

Character Devices

Another class of devices are character devices that typically have a protocol defined using which the driver can communicate with the device. The subtle difference is that the communication happens by sending and receiving single characters, which is usually a byte or an octet. Many serial port devices like keyboards, some sensor devices, and microcontrollers follow this mechanism.

The protocols used by the different devices (block devices or character devices) could vary from one to another. There are three main categories of I/O protocols that are used.

Special Instruction I/O

There could be specific CPU instructions that are custom developed for communicating with and controlling the I/O devices. For example, there could be a CPU-specific protocol to communicate with the embedded controller. This may be needed for faster and efficient communication. However, such type of I/Os are special and smaller in number.

Memory-Mapped I/O

The most common form of I/O protocol is memory-mapped I/O (MMIO). As we discussed in the "Memory Management" section, the device and OS agree on a common address range carved out by the OS, and the I/O device makes reads and writes from/to this space to communicate to the OS.

OS components such as drivers will communicate using this interface to talk to the device. MMIO is also an effective mechanism for data transfer that can be implemented without using up precious CPU cycles. Hence, it is used to enable high-speed communication for network and graphics devices that require high data transfer rates due to the volume of data being passed.

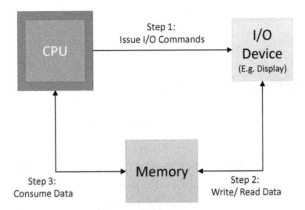

Figure 4-12. *Memory-Mapped I/O Flow in a Graphics Device Example*

Figure 4-12 depicts the case where the graphics driver acts as the I/O device and a memory-mapped location is used to share and communicate to the graphics device.

Direct Memory Access (DMA)

As we discussed earlier, there could be devices that run at a slower speed than supported by the CPU or the bus it is connected on. In this case, the device can leverage DMA. Here, the OS grants authority to another controller, usually referred to as the direct memory access controller, to interrupt the CPU after a specific data transfer is complete. The devices running at a smaller rate can communicate back to the DMA controller after completing its operation.

Most OSs also handle additional specific device classes, blocking and nonblocking I/Os, and other I/O controls. As a programmer, you could be interacting with devices that may perform caching (an intermediate layer that acts as a buffer to report data faster) and have different error reporting mechanisms, protocols, and so on.

Next, let's consider the difference between a polled and an interrupt-driven I/O.

Polled vs. Interrupt I/Os

Consider our temperature device discussed previously. If the device supports a polled I/O mechanism, the typical flow would involve requesting the device for temperature by issuing the command and filling the data field. At this point, the host system could wait for the operation to complete. In this case, it could be a blocked I/O call and a synchronous operation. However, it may not be efficient to block the execution. So, alternatively, the host system may issue a call and check the response at a later point in time if the operation has been completed. These could be implemented as a polled and an interrupt-driven I/O as shown in Figure 4-13.

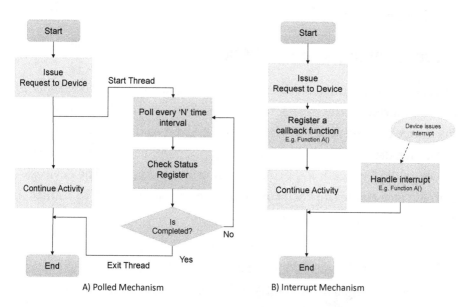

Figure 4-13. *Example Polled vs. Interrupt-Driven I/O Flow*

One mechanism would be for the host to poll the device and check the status of the operation. There is usually a status register that determines if the device has completed the operation. This is a common I/O flow for some devices as shown in Figure 4-13 (A).

Another mechanism would be to use the interrupt-driven mechanism. In this case, the request for operation is issued to the device. A callback function is also defined that needs to get called when the operation is completed. The device would continue and complete the operation and raise an interrupt once done as shown in Figure 4-13 (B). The callback function would be called appropriately to handle the interrupt. The callback function is also called as the ISR (Interrupt Service Routine), and as the name suggests, it services the interrupt. As a programmer, it is important to keep in mind that these ISRs are short-lived and lightweight and need to service the interrupt raised as quickly as possible.

I/O and Performance

The I/O subsystem plays a major factor in the overall performance of the system. As a software programmer, some of the operations done by your program could inadvertently impact the performance of the system. For example, a program could have multiple context switches arising due to the delays, responsiveness, and performance of the devices on the system. This may lead to an overall impact on the performance of your application. An application performing frequent writes to the disk or making many requests for continuous memory allocation can lead to excessive page swapping. A program could request for memory and may inadvertently not free up the memory requested after usage. These can cause memory leaks that may result in lower available memory and eventually impact the system performance. Also, requests for large blocks of contiguous memory may also have an impact since the memory subsystem may have to swap memory to accommodate the same.

115

A programmer would need to be cognizant of the I/O subsystem and its limitations in terms of performance expectations, limits/boundaries, and potential impacts. This is required since it may not only affect their application but could also affect the overall platform eventually.

Synchronization Concepts

Given there are devices and apps that must run together, access to hardware needs to be properly synchronized. There could be situations where more than one application may want to communicate to the same hardware device and the hardware device may not support concurrent access. It is important to know a few basics about how the OS uses synchronization to avoid potential conflicts. For this, let's start with the concepts of atomicity, critical sections, and locks.

Consider a multi-threaded application where a function is incrementing a global static variable:

```
count++; // count is a location in RAM
```

The preceding statement can be decomposed into three operations, which include fetching the value of count, incrementing the value of count in a local register, and then storing the updated value back to memory. However, as we saw earlier in this chapter, the thread that was executing this instruction could have been swapped in the middle of this operation. At the same time, there could be another thread that could be swapped in and may try to increment count. This is depicted in Figure 4-14 where Thread A was in the middle of incrementing while another thread tried to read the value of count. Ideally, Thread B should be able to access the count variable only after the operation in Thread A was completed.

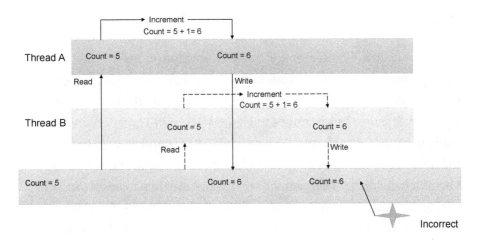

Figure 4-14. Example of Increment Operation (count++) Across Threads

If more than one thread tries to increment count at the same time, we may get unexpected results at any of the three steps we've described in the preceding. Such bugs are quite difficult to recreate and locate. This is an example where we need atomicity in instruction execution. Atomicity, as the name suggests, is a group of instructions that may need to be executed together as if they were a single instruction. The OS attempts to protect us from interrupting individual instructions while they are being executed.

Critical Sections

In multi-threaded applications, if one thread tries to change the value of shared data at the same time as another thread tries to read the value, there could be a race condition across threads. In this case, the result can be unpredictable. The access to such shared variables via shared memory, files, ports, and other I/O resources needs to be synchronized to protect it from being corrupted. In order to support this, the operating system provides mutexes and semaphores to coordinate access to these shared resources.

Mutex

A mutex is used for implementing mutual exclusion: either of the participating processes or threads can have the key (mutex) and proceed with their work. The other one would have to wait until the one holding the mutex finishes. As we can see in Figure 4-15, both Threads A and B would like to access a shared resource such as a file and write to it. Thread A initiates a request to acquire a lock before it can access the file. Once the lock is acquired, it finishes its operations on the file and then releases the lock. During this time, Thread B will not be able to access the file. Once completed, Thread B can follow the same procedure to access the shared resource.

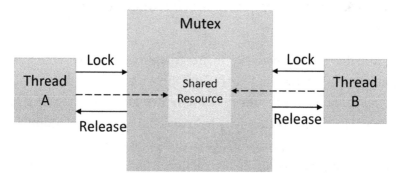

Figure 4-15. *Example Mutex*

A sample pseudo-code of the same implementation is shown in the following. As we can see, both threads try to acquire the lock before accessing the shared resource, that is, count in this case:

```
incrementCount()
{
    mutex_lock(&COUNT_MUTEX);
    count = count + 1;
    mutex_unlock(&COUNT_MUTEX);
}
```

Semaphore

A semaphore is a generalized mutex. A binary semaphore can assume a value of 0/1 and can be used to perform locks to certain critical sections. It is usually helpful to batch lock resource requests for better performance. As we can see in Figure 4-16, each of the threads A, B, C, and D requires access to the critical shared resource. When each of the threads requests to acquire the lock, the semaphore increments a counter and also maintains a waiting list of threads on the shared resource. Typically semaphores also expose two functions wait() and signal() that may be used to send notifications to threads appropriately.

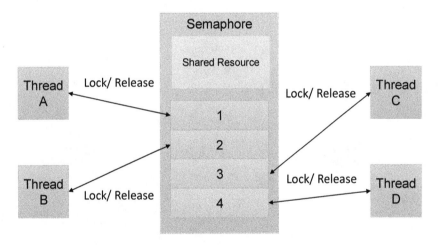

Figure 4-16. *Example Semaphore*

Now that we have seen how mutexes and semaphores work, we will go over another concept called deadlocks that may happen when the OS attempts to synchronize the operations on the system.

Deadlocks

In general, when we access a resource, we don't always know all the ways other parts of the system may also access that resource. The OS manages this resource access, but there could be certain situations where a set of processes become blocked because each process is holding a resource and waiting for another resource acquired by some other process. This is called as a deadlock. As we can see in Figure 4-17, Process A holds Resource 1 and requires Resource 2. However, Process B already is holding Resource 2, but requires Resource 1. Unless either of them releases their resource, neither of the processes may be able to move forward with the execution.

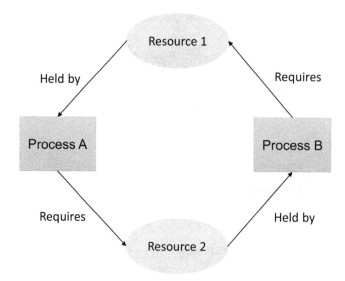

Figure 4-17. *Example of a Deadlock*

To elaborate from Figure 4-17, a deadlock can arise if the following four conditions hold:

- Mutual Exclusion: There is at least one resource on the system that is not shareable. This means that only one process can access this at any point in time. In the preceding example, Resources 1 and 2 can be accessed by only one process at any time.

- Hold and Wait: A process is holding at least one resource and is waiting for other resources to proceed with its action. In the preceding example, both Processes A and B are holding at least one resource.

- No Preemption: A resource cannot be forcefully taken from a process unless released automatically.

- Circular Wait: A set of processes are waiting for each other in circular form. As we can see in Figure 4-17, the arrows form a circular loop.

There are various mechanisms available to handle deadlocks using mutexes and semaphores that we discussed earlier along with additional algorithms to detect, avoid, and prevent deadlocks on the system. As a programmer, you would want to use these synchronization mechanisms.

To summarize, the I/O subsystem plays a critical role in the overall performance of the system. Memory management, interrupt responses, handling of I/O serializations, synchronizations, contentions, and so on play an important role in the overall performance of the system. Defining them, tuning and optimizing these are a major challenge for any operating system. There are various adaptive methodologies and runtime optimizations that various OS vendors invest in and try to adopt. These will continue to evolve for the better usage of our hardware.

File Systems

Applications often need to read and write files to achieve their goals. We leverage the OS to create, read, and write such files on the system. We depend on the OS to maintain and manage files on the system. OS file systems have two main components to facilitate file management:

1. Directory Service: There is a need to uniquely manage files in a structured manner, manage access, and provide Read-Write-Edit controls on the file system. This is taken care by a layer called as the **directory service**.

2. Storage Service: There is a need to communicate to the underlying hardware such as the disk. This is managed by a **storage service** that abstracts different types of storage devices on the system.

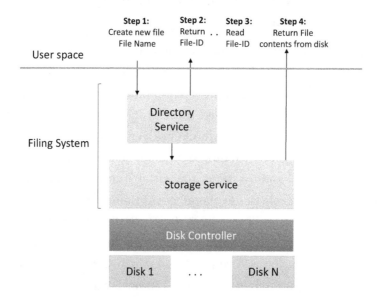

Figure 4-18. *File System Overview with File Access Process*

As shown in Figure 4-18, when a new file is created, the file name and path are passed to the directory service, which creates a unique file ID. This reference is used later to read contents back from the file using the storage service.

We will start with file concepts and then proceed to the functionality details.

File Concepts

From the perspective of the user, a file is a collection of related data that is stored together and can be accessed using a unique file ID usually referred as the file name. These files can be represented internally by different methods. For example, there could be .bin files in Windows, which only represent a sequence of bytes. There could be other structured contents with headers and specific sections in the file. For example, an EXE is also a file format in Windows with specific headers, a body, and controls in place. There are also many application-specific files, with their own formats. It is up to the programmer to define and identify if they require a custom file format for their application or if they can leverage a standard or common file format such as the JavaScript Object Notation (JSON) or the Extensible Markup Language (XML).

As a programmer, it may be important to know the attributes of the file before accessing it. The common attributes of any file include the location of the file, file extension, size, access controls, and some history of operations done on the file, to name a few. Some of these are part of the so-called file control block, which a user has access to via the OS. Most OSs expose APIs using which the programmer can access the details in the file control block. For the user, these are exposed on the graphical user interface via built-in tools shipped with the OS.

Directory Namespace

The operating system defines a logical ordering of different files on the system based on the usage and underlying storage services. One of the criteria most OSs adopt is to structure their directory service to locate files efficiently.

As shown in Figure 4-19, most OSs organize their files in a hierarchical form with files organized inside folders. Each folder in this case is a directory. This structure is called as the directory namespace. The directory service and namespace have additional capabilities such as searches by size, type, access levels, and so on. The directory namespaces can be multileveled and adaptive in modern OSs as we can see in the following folder structure with folders created inside another folder.

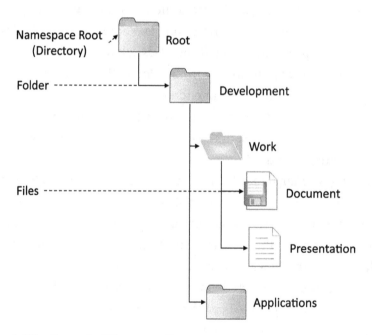

Figure 4-19. *Sample Directory Structure*

As a programmer, you should be aware of a few additional basic concepts from the file system point of view. We will discuss them in this section.

Access Control

There are different access levels that can be applied at file and directory levels. For example, we may not want a user-mode application running with a normal user credential to be able to make changes to some OS files/ services. The OS provides different access control IDs and permissions to different users on the system. Also, each file may also have different levels of permissions to Read, Write, Modify, and so on. For example, there may be specific files that we may want anyone to be able to access and Read but not Write and Modify. The file system provides and manages the controls to all files when accessed at runtime. These may also be helpful when more than one user is using the same system.

Concurrency and Cleanup Control

There are many cases when the OS needs to ensure that a file is not moved or deleted when it is in use. For example, if a user is making changes to a file, the OS needs to ensure that the same file cannot be moved or deleted by another application or process. In this case, the OS would cause the attempt to move or delete the file to fail with an appropriate error code. As a programmer, it is appropriate to access a file with the required access level and mode (Read/Write). This also helps to be in line with the concurrency needs of the OS and guards against inconsistent updates.

The OS also needs to be able to periodically clear temporarily created files that may no longer be required for the functioning of the system. This is typically done using a garbage collector on the system. Many OSs mark unused files over a period of time and have additional settings that are exposed, which the user can set to clean up files from specified locations automatically.

Overall, the file system provides access, access controls, and protection mechanisms to files in the directory namespace. The programmer needs to be aware of the protections and have the right access controls (privileges) to interact with the file system successfully.

Access and Protection

If we have a system that is used by only one user without any access, networked or otherwise, to other systems, there may still not be assurance that the contents in the system are protected. There is still a need to protect the program resources from other applications. Also, there may be a need to protect critical devices on the system.

In practice, there is always a need to connect and share resources and data between systems. Hence, it is important to protect these resources accordingly. The OS provides APIs that help with access control and protection. Let's start with some of the concepts.

Rings: User Mode and Kernel Mode

We briefly covered user-mode and kernel-mode processes in the "Scheduling" section. One of the reasons the separation between user mode and kernel mode is implemented by most OSs is that it ensures different privilege levels are granted to programs, based on which mode they run in.

As shown in Figure 4-20, an abstract OS divides the program execution privileges into different rings. Internally, programs running in specific rings are associated with specific access levels and privileges. For example, applications and user-mode services running in Ring 3 would not be able to access the hardware directly. The drivers running on the Ring 0 level would have the highest privileges and access to the hardware on the system. In practice, most OSs only leverage two rings, which are Ring 0 and Ring 3.

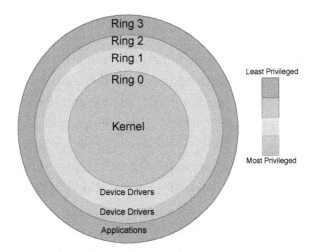

Figure 4-20. *Applications, Drivers, and Rings in an Operating System*

Virtualization

Consider the scenario where it may be required to have multiple closed environments that assume to have dedicated access to the resources on the platform. Operating systems and modern hardware provide a feature called virtualization that, you guessed it, virtualizes the hardware such that each calling environment believes it has the dedicated access it needs to function.

Virtualization is delivered via so-called virtual machines (VMs). A VM has its own **guest** OS, which may be the same as or different from the underlying **host** OS. A user can launch a VM, much like running any other program, and log into the guest OS. The host OS provides a hypervisor, which manages the access to the hardware. The guest OS is usually unaware of the internals and passes any resource/hardware requests to the host OS. The user can completely customize their VM and perform all their actions on this VM without affecting the host OS or any other VM on the system. At a high level, VMs help effectively utilize the hardware resources and are used heavily in server and cloud deployments.

Protection

There could be different security threats that may arise during the usage of a computer. These could attempt to access different critical resources on the platform such as data, compute, memory, and so on. The operating system needs to be able to detect any such attempts and potentially mitigate them. A threat could be any local or remote program that may be attempting to compromise the integrity of the resources in the system. To mitigate this, modern OSs usually implement checks to detect and protect against such incursions.

The most common protection would be to authorize the requester and apply authentication to any new request to the system. For example, when a request is made to a critical resource, the operating system would verify the user request (which is called as authentication) and their approved access levels (which is called authorization) and controls before providing access to a critical resource on the system. The OS may also have Access Control Lists (ACLs) that contain mapping of system resources to different permission levels. This is used internally before the OS grants permissions to any resource. Additionally, the OS may also provide services to encrypt and verify certificates that help with enhancing the security and protection of the system itself.

To summarize, the programmer needs to be aware of the various access controls and protection mechanisms in place and use the right protocols and OS services to successfully access resources on the system.

User Interface and Shell

Although the user interface (UI) is not part of the OS kernel itself, this is typically considered to be an integral part of the OS. That said, many OSs support different UIs, many of which are provided by third parties, for instance.

There can be multiple user interfaces for the OS all being implemented either as a text-based interface (e.g., MS-DOS) or a graphical-based interface (e.g., Microsoft Windows 10, macOS, etc.). The graphical user interface is the rich set of graphical front-end interfaces and functionalities provided by the OS for the user to interact with the computer. There could be an alternate simpler interface through a command line shell interface that most OSs also provide for communication. This is a text-based interface. It is common for programmers to use the shell interface instead of the GUI for quickly traversing through the file system and interacting with the OS. It requires the user to be aware of the commands and have the knowledge of the underlying OS implementations to be able to use it efficiently.

It is important for the software developer to be aware that the user interface and the shell interface may have an impact on their choice of programing language, handling of command line arguments, handling of the standard input-output pipes and interfacing with OS policies, and so on. Please note that the user interface and the features can be quite varied and different from each OS to another and are beyond the scope of this book.

Some OS Specifics

All OSs have features that may be unique to them. For example, UNIX has its own level of file abstraction and a hierarchical namespace. It handles heavyweight processes uniquely and supports pipes and signals for IPCs. Some of the recent UNIX enhancements provide additional capabilities and fixes across many of the IPC mechanisms.

Similarly, Windows NT has a layered architecture with Win32 APIs and a contained Windows Driver Framework (WDF) for driver development. Windows also has its unique way of handling plug and play (PnP) of devices on the system, power management, and I/O subsystem. Some of these may vary from one Windows version to the other as well.

From a programmer point of view, most of the basic concepts remain similar across these OSs. However, there could be few modifications and enhancements that you need to be aware of for your code to work across OSs. For example, the paths used to access files on the system or APIs referenced may be dependent on the OS/shell; and if you don't code for these situations, your code may not work as expected across OSs. You may want to keep these in mind at development. Further details are beyond the scope of this book.

Summary

In this chapter, we have described how the operating system forms an integral part of the system providing numerous capabilities including interaction with hardware and users and managing programs. OSs employ many design considerations and strategies based on which the OS abstracts and ensures seamless usage of the system.

As a software developer, you could be part of a larger ecosystem that could delve into device management, networking, web development, data management, and many other domains. The interfaces between the different domains and the way the operating system streamlines the operations between them are important for a software developer to comprehend and make meaningful decisions. Understanding these fundamentals helps in applying them at the various stages of software development ranging from architecture, design, deployment, and debug by taking the right choices.

References and Further Reading

- Arpaci-Dusseau, R. H.-D (2018). *Three Easy Pieces.* Arpaci-Dusseau Books. CITATION Rem18\l 1033. Arpaci-Dusseau, 2018

- Avi Silberschatz, P. B. (2012). *Operating System Concepts (Ninth Edition).* John Wiley & Sons, Inc. CITATION Avi12\l 1033. Avi Silberschatz, 2012

CHAPTER 5

Computer Networks and Distributed Systems

So far, we have discussed the computer systems in isolation. Computers need to talk to each other to enable communication with other systems to enable higher-value services. When we talk about a set of computers communicating over a network, we are describing a distributed system. In this chapter, we will discuss how this happens.

History and Evolution of Networks and the Internet

Since the beginning of electronic computers, humans have had the desire to connect them. The US Department of Defense ARPANET was one of the earliest networks. By 1971, ARPANET was a 15-node network.

Roberts and Merrill proposed a common "messaging protocol" for heterogeneous computers to have a common language for sharing messages. Heterogeneous networks are defined as being made up of different computers, from different vendors. Wesley Clark, another researcher at ARPANET, proposed a two-layer approach, of an interface

© Paul D. Crutcher, Neeraj Kumar Singh, and Peter Tiegs 2021
P. D. Crutcher et al., *Essential Computer Science*,
https://doi.org/10.1007/978-1-4842-7107-0_5

layer and a communications layer. Hosts would provide the user interface, initiate the connection, and maintain the connection. And a communications layer of Interface Message Processors (IMPs) would move the data through the subnets to other hosts.

IMPs would break messages from the host into 8096-bit packets. A packet can be thought of as an envelope; it is a discrete set of bits that contain the message, or part of a message. A packet header contains the routing information and can be thought of as the address on the envelope. The IMP protocol added a common header that included source, destination, and control information. Routing is determining where to send a packet, so that it arrives at its proper destination. In IMPs, routing to the destination was not done by a central router; rather, each IMP kept a table of the routes with the amount of time it takes to send one of these packets. To ensure the arrival of the packets, an acknowledgement message was sent from the receiving IMP, and a checksum was used to verify the data was uncorrupted. If, after a certain period of time, the packet was not acknowledged, it would be sent again.

By 1971, a third layer had been added to the network stack, now application, host, and communications. Also, by 1971, the first application, a remote login program called telnet, was generally available. The File Transfer Protocol (FTP) and email were soon added and generally available by 1972. In the spring of 1972, ARPANET was demonstrated for the first time at the first International Conference on Computer and Communications (ICCC). The ARPANET that was demonstrated in 1972 was not the Internet though. It was a single network of 15 computers with one killer app in the form of email. What was learned in the development of ARPANET, however, led to the creation of the Internet.

Robert Kahn extended the work from ARPANET to see if the techniques could be applied to radio for both terrestrial transmission and satellite transmission. The biggest impact of this research was applied to local area networks.

ARPANET typically used leased phone lines to connect from computer to computer; however, in Hawaii, the phone lines were too noisy for clean data transmission. So ALOHAnet used radio to transmit the packets. ALOHAnet used two radio channels: one for machine data and one for user data. As you can imagine, without knowing when a transmission would be received, it was likely that two systems would transmit at the same time and collide with each other. It was impossible to know when to transmit to avoid a collision on the channel. ALOHAnet provided an elegant solution by not trying to avoid collisions. Recognizing that collisions would occur, the ALOHAnet researchers created an algorithm that would select a random time to wait and retransmit.

Robert Metcalfe improved on this algorithm with subsequent transmission collisions that would increase the random wait time exponentially to back off of a congested channel. Metcalfe applied this radio transmission technique to transmission on wires. Where transmitting data over radio at the time could carry thousands of bits per second, the transmissions over wires could transmit millions. Transmitting data on wires with this technique was named Ethernet.

Ethernet became the standard for data transmission for a local area network (LAN). By 1982, Ethernet products were commercially available for personal computers.

Robert Kahn and Vincent Cerf, both computer science researchers on ARPANET, created the Internet architecture. The Internet architecture was more flexible and more distributed than the architecture of ARPANET. The Internet architecture was adopted by not only the Internet itself but many other networks.

In 1973, Vincent Cerf organized a seminar to design the Internet host protocol, the Transmission Control Protocol (TCP). Cerf and Kahn asked the questions what would be the best protocol for unreliable networks and what would be the best way to connect different networks. Both Cerf and Metcalfe, as well as Gerard Le Lann, collaborated on TCP; as a result, TCP reflected the Ethernet protocol. TCP would be able to handle collisions and out-of-order packet reception. The second question of how to connect different networks had two possible answers. The first possible answer was to continue doing what had been done, which is let each network have its own protocol and then translate between protocols at the network edge. Cerf and Khan realized this would not scale as the number of networks grew, so they pushed for the second possible answer, to have a common protocol, TCP. The advantages of a common protocol, such as a common address space and transparency of the network boundaries, were worth the cost of needing to upgrade legacy networks.

To connect to other LANs and potentially translate between different network protocols, Cerf proposed a special kind of computer called a gateway. A gateway would be connected to two or more networks, and those gateways would maintain routing tables between the networks. This allows the local networks to connect to other networks and eventually be part of the Internet without having total knowledge of the Internet.

TCP required that all packets were reliably delivered, but this was not needed in every case. In some cases, for instance, if you are broadcasting a message out to lots of subscribers and don't care if they get it or not, an unreliable protocol makes more sense. As such, in 1978, Vincent Cerf, Jon Postel, and Dan Cohen proposed that TCP was split into two protocols, TCP and IP. TCP was still responsible for reliable delivery, and IP was for simply passing packets between machines. This reduced the complexity of gateways, because they now only needed to handle IP.

By the end of the 1970s, TCP/IP had been developed and by the early 1980s had become a de facto standard for computer-to-computer communication. At the time, it was not the only standard floating around. A group of public telephone companies and communication equipment manufacturers had developed a standard called X.25 that largely overlapped with TCP/IP. X.25 varied from TCP/IP in that it defined network switching nodes to make virtual circuits between computers during the communication sessions.

Many in the community saw that X.25 was in direct competition with TCP/IP and a threat to open networks. Both network protocols were used during this period, with commercial networks using X.25, while the ARPA Internet used TCP/IP and private networks used a mix of X.25 and TCP/IP. While the debate about how to connect these disparate networks continued, the International Organization for Standardization (ISO) was focusing on computer manufacturers. To help keep the emerging network standards open, ISO created the Open Systems Interconnection (OSI) project.

Because networking computers were still new, ISO did not want to specify specific protocols or standards. Instead, they provided a standard model for creating network models. ISO based their model on the layering scheme that had been created by ARPANET. The OSI model consists of seven layers: physical, link, network, transport, session, presentation, and application (Figure 5-1). The layering scheme allowed ISO standards for network protocols to be slotted into the appropriate layer. A side effect of this layered approach to the network model was that it shaped the thinking of network protocols.

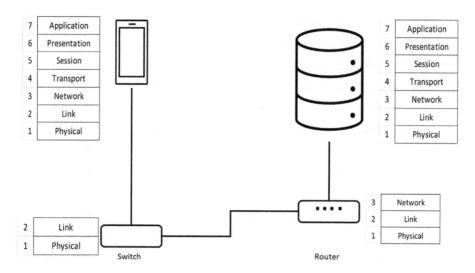

Figure 5-1. *OSI Layered Model Showing Layers Used for Connection*

Throughout the 1980s, the Internet grew from a small set of networks mostly related to defense research to an enormous network of computers and users. The Internet was transferred from military to civilian control. At the same time, the personal computer revolution was happening. One growing capability of personal computers was the ability to connect to other users through dial-up modems and bulletin board systems (BBSs). BBSs were sometimes connected to FidoNet, a network of bulletin board systems.

In 1989, Tim Berners-Lee invented the HyperText Markup Language (HTML) and the Hypertext Transfer Protocol (HTTP). This was the beginning of the World Wide Web as we know it. In 1993, Marc Andreessen and Eric Bina created a graphical user interface web browser for the National Center of Supercomputing Applications (NCSA) called Mosaic. The Mosaic client used HTTP to connect to servers on the Internet to download and display HTML content. Web browsers have continued to evolve as one of the primary clients of the Internet Protocols.

The World Wide Web Consortium (W3C) was founded in 1994 by Tim Berners-Lee, with a mission to lead the World Wide Web to its full potential by defining protocols and guidelines to ensure long-term growth of the Web.

Protocols: Stateful and Stateless

Protocols are the language used to communicate between computing systems on a network called nodes. The protocols carry the information about the connection as well as the content. Protocols define the rules of how to communicate between nodes. The protocol algorithm defines the rules such as who speaks next and what is expected. A protocol is implemented by a header containing the required data and an algorithm that utilizes that data.

Network protocols can be either stateful or stateless. Stateful protocols keep track of the connection between the two nodes as part of the protocol data itself. Stateless protocols do not track the state in the protocol, so, in general, there is no relation from one message to the next. There are advantages to both types of protocols, as we discuss in the following.

Internet Protocol (IP): TCP and UDP

The Internet Protocol suite handles the connections between the host systems on the Internet, covering the transport and network levels in the OSI model. The Transmission Control Protocol (TCP) is used for connection-oriented data traffic. The User Datagram Protocol (UDP) is used for connectionless data traffic. Connectionless data traffic is data that is sent but not guaranteed to be received by another node. We will describe why this is done in the UDP section. The underlying Internet Protocol (IP) provides the methods to instruct and route the traffic on the network. The current version of IP is IPv6; however, IPv4 is still in heavy use. One of the key differences between IPv4 and IPv6 is the available addressable space in the IP address. IPv4 has 32-bit IP addresses with both the source and destination host addresses and has a 20-byte header (Figure 5-2). IPv6 has 128-bit IP addresses, again with both source and destination, and has a 40-byte header (Figure 5-3).

0 1 2 3	4 5 6 7	8 9 10 11 12 13 14 15	16 17 18 19 20 21 22 23 24 25 26 27 28 29 30 31
version	header length	type of service	total length
Identification			0 DF MF fragment offset
time to live		protocol	header checksum
32-bit source IPv4 Address			
32-bit destination IPv4 Address			

Figure 5-2. *IPv4 Header (32 Bits per Row)*

0 1 2 3	4 5 6 7	8 9 10 11 12 13 14 15 16 17 18 19	20 21 22 23	24 25 26 27 28 29 30 31
version	priority	flow label		
payload length			next header	hop limit
128-bit source IPV6 Address				
128-bit destination IPv6 Address				

Figure 5-3. *IPv6 Header (32 Bits per Row)*

The Transmission Control Protocol, TCP, sits on top of IP (Figure 5-4). TCP is the same regardless of whether it uses IPv4 or IPv6. TCP is a connection-oriented protocol in that it provides a byte stream for user processes that is both full duplex and reliable. TCP is reliable because it guarantees the data is sequenced and can be reassembled in the same order it was sent. Many of the most common application protocols such as FTP, HTTP, and ISMP sit on top of TCP. TCP provides features like acknowledgement and timeouts to increase reliability. TCP is also full duplex, which means that data can simultaneously be sent and received by both endpoints on a single connection. TCP keeps track of state information such as the sequence numbers of the message segments.

0	1	2	3	4	5	6	7	8	9	10	11	12	13	14	15	16	17	18	19	20	21	22	23	24	25	26	27	28	29	30	31
source port																destination port															
length																checksum															

Figure 5-4. *TCP Header (32 Bits per Row)*

TCP defines a connection algorithm that is illustrated in Figure 5-5. First, a client will send a synchronization (SYN) message to the server with a sequence number (j). If and when that is received by the server, the server will send both its own synchronization (SYN) with a sequence number (k) and an acknowledgement (ACK) with the client's sequence number increased (j+1). Finally, if and when the client receives this message, it will respond back with an acknowledgement (ACK) with the server's sequence number increased (k+1). Once this handshake is done, then the client and server are connected and can communicate.

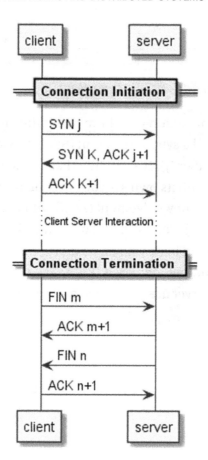

Figure 5-5. *TCP Connect and Disconnect*

When the client is done communicating with the server, it can terminate the connection by sending a finish (FIN) message and sequence number (m). The server responds with an acknowledgement (ACK) and sequence number (m+1) and then its own finish (FIN) message. Finally, the client responds with an acknowledgement (ACK) of the server's finish message, after which the client and server are not connected.

UDP or the User Datagram Protocol is the other part of the Internet Protocol suite. Unlike TCP, UDP is a connectionless protocol; this means that UDP can send a message to multiple receivers without disconnecting from one receiver (Figure 5-6). This also means that there is no formal relationship between the senders and receivers, so receipt of the data is not guaranteed. UDP is typically used where performance and speed are more important than reliability. UDP messages are often referred to as datagrams. DHCP (Dynamic Host Configuration Protocol), RIP (Routing Information Protocol), and DNS (Domain Name System) are examples of protocols that are on top of UDP.

0	1	2	3	4	5	6	7	8	9	10	11	12	13	14	15	16	17	18	19	20	21	22	23	24	25	26	27	28	29	30	31
source port																destination port															
sequence number																															
acknowledged number																															
header length					unused							urg	ack	psh	rst	syn	fin	receive window															
checksum																urgent data pointer															
options																															

Figure 5-6. *UDP Header (32 Bits per Row)*

Host, IP Address, MAC Address, Port, Socket

The computers that are the various endpoints in the network are generically referred to as hosts. Hosts may have one or more physical layer connections to the network such as Ethernet adapters, Wi-Fi cards, or wireless WAN adapters. The link layer is this direct node-to-node connection from a physical connection on one system to a single other system. The MAC (media access control) address is the link layer address of these physical connections. The MAC address is a unique 48-bit number assigned to each device. With 48 bits, there is an addressable space for over 200 trillion devices on the network. The IEEE manages the assignment of MAC addresses to manufacturers of network equipment to prevent collisions of MAC addresses.

One or more IP addresses at the network layer can be assigned to the link layer MAC address. For IPv4, the IP address is a 32-bit number that is typically written as four dot-separated (between each byte) fields with values ranging from 0 to 255. With a 32-bit number, the addressable space is about 4 billion possible IP addresses. With the explosion of the number of hosts on the Internet, especially Internet of Things (IoT) hosts, this 4 billion number is too small. An IPv6 address is a 128-bit number typically written as eight fields of four hexadecimal (16-bit/2-byte) digits separated by colons. 128 bits provides a sufficiently large address space for the future of the Internet. A loopback IP address represents the device to itself. The loopback addresses are 127.0.0.1 and 0:0:0:0:0:0:0:1 for IPv4 and IPv6, respectively. Multiple services or processes can run on the same host concurrently by using either TCP or UDP. Each service listens on a port number, which is a 16-bit number. Each service must have a unique port number to be accessible on a given host. When a client or a peer needs to connect to a particular service or peer, it needs to specify not only the IP address but the port that the service process is listening on. Sockets are an API (application programming interface) for connecting to network services. A socket is bound to a port and allows a program to send and receive data with another program. The Internet Assigned Numbers Authority (IANA) assigns ports and port ranges to various applications (Table 5-1) to avoid conflicts.

Table 5-1. *IANA Common Port Numbers and Ranges*

Port	Description
20	FTP Data
21	FTP Control
22	SSH
23	Telnet
25	Simple Mail Transfer
80	HTTP

(*continued*)

Table 5-1. (*continued*)

Port	Description
92	Network Printing Protocol
443	HTTPS
546	DHCP Client
547	DHCP Server
631	Internet Printing Protocol
8080	HTTP Alternate
1-1023	IANA well-known ports
1024-49151	IANA registered ports
49152-65535	IANA dynamic or private ports

DNS and DHCP

IP addresses are a great way of uniquely identifying hosts on the network, but it can be very difficult for humans to understand and remember the addresses of various hosts. The Domain Name Service (DNS) is a protocol to map human-understandable names to IP addresses. DNS sits on top of UDP. DNS servers maintain a mapping of domain names or human-understandable addresses to hosts on the Internet and the corresponding IP addresses. A DNS server will respond to a DNS resolution request with the IP address (Figure 5-7). If the DNS server does not have a matching name to IP address, it forwards the request up to a more authoritative DNS server, which may forward the request to other DNS servers. Once there is a name match, the IP address is returned to the original requestor. The remaining interactions between those hosts will be done with IP addresses.

DNS names follow a specific set of rules. The names must end in a top-level domain (TLD) such as .com or .org. Various countries each have top-level domains. Preceding the top-level domain is a subdomain. This is usually the name of the organization that manages the host. Proceeding the subdomain and top-level domain is an arbitrary name for the specific host. Domain names are registered by a domain name registrar under the supervision of ICANN, the Internet Corporation for Assigned Names and Numbers.

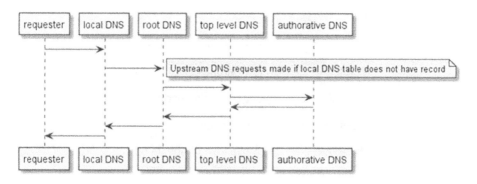

Figure 5-7. *Domain Name Lookup Sequence*

The Dynamic Host Configuration Protocol or DHCP is a protocol to dynamically assign IP addresses to hosts on a LAN or IP segment. It is very common to use DHCP on local area networks so a person does not have to explicitly assign IP addresses to every host on the network.

With DHCP, the host sends out a DHCP service discovery message on the network. When a DHCP host receives a service discovery message, it responds with an IP address for the requesting system, the network mask, and the IP address lease time.

A network mask is a bit pattern that indicates which bits in the IP address cannot change. This indicates the range of possible IP addresses the host can reach. The network mask is sometimes called the subnet mask because it defines the subnet that the host is part of. A subnet is one or more hosts connected to a router. As an example (Figure 5-8), we have two subnets 143.11.38.0/24 and 143.11.40.0/24, where the first 24 bits or three fields of the IP addresses in the subnets will be the same.

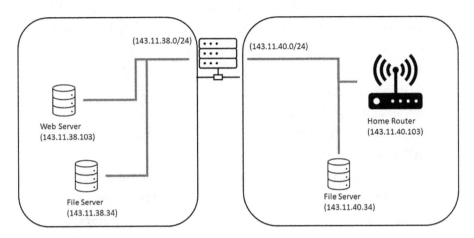

Figure 5-8. *Two Subnets Connected to a Router*

The DHCP lease time is how long the requesting client will have that IP address before needing to request a new one. Once the client selects the IP address, it will respond back to the DHCP server with a request for that IP address. Finally, the DHCP server will respond, acknowledging that the client is associated with that IP address. In addition to the IP address information, a DHCP server can also provide the address to a DNS server.

Proxy, Firewall, Routing

Routers are computers that have the responsibility of moving network packets through the network. A router does this by forwarding packets from an inbound link to an outbound link. A router uses a forwarding table to determine which outbound link to send the packet, by inspecting the destination IP address in the packet.

The forwarding table is kept up to date with the current network topology with the Routing Information Protocol (RIP). RIP is a UDP with datagrams from other routers and systems. Because RIP is a connectionless UDP, the packets sometimes get lost. This is ok because the routing table will just get updated with the next RIP datagram. RIP provides a distance measurement to a router, by counting how many hops (number of routers it passes through) between the source and destination.

Another routing protocol is OSPF (Open Shortest Path First), which provides information to routers to build a complete map of the network topology, allowing packet forwarding to be based on a shortest path to the destination. OSPF is used by upper-tier Internet Service Providers, ISPs, where RIP is used inside enterprise networks.

The next routing protocol is the Border Gateway Protocol (BGP). BGP is used by subnets to advertise that subnet is part of the Internet.

Network Address Translation (NAT) does a similar job to routers of taking incoming packages and sending them out to a specific destination. Private IP addresses are IP addresses that can be used in multiple local area networks without conflicting as they cannot be routed out to the broader Internet. This is typically the type of IP address a DHCP server will serve up. To send and receive packets to and from these private networks, a NAT table is used to associate a private network IP address and port to a public IP address and port. For instance (Figure 5-9), you may be running a web server on your private network at 10.0.0.11 on port 80 and an FTP server at 10.0.0.9 on port 22 with NAT to your ISP-assigned address 143.11.38.34. The Internet only sees one device 143.11.38.34 and can send packets to that device. The NAT will inspect the packet it receives at 143.11.38.34 to check the port destination and then forward that packet to one of the two machines on the private network.

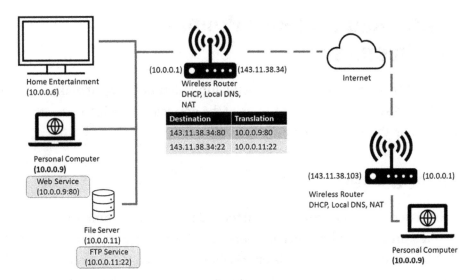

Figure 5-9. *Typical Network with DHCP and Network Address Translation*

A firewall works similarly to a NAT in that it inspects the incoming packets. Depending on certain criteria, it will either forward that packet or drop it. The destination application and port number are common rules that are set up in firewalls. Other rules include destination IP addresses and hostnames.

A proxy server is another service similar to a firewall in that it usually is part of the edge of a network before packets are sent out to the broader Internet to help secure your traffic. Even with encryption of the data, with TCP/IP, the headers are not encrypted, so your source and destination IP addresses are exposed. If you want to hide your source address, a proxy service will replace your source address with a proxy address and send it onto the destination. The destination will then respond back to the proxy server, which will reassemble the received packet with the original source address as the destination of the response.

Distributed Systems: Prominent Architectures

Now that we have looked at some of the fundamentals of what makes up a distributed system, let's look at some of the application architectures that are built on these network configurations.

Client Server

A client-server architecture is one of the oldest and most common architectures you will see on a network. In this architecture, you will see a centralized server that multiple clients connect to in order to accomplish a task. Many of the common Internet applications use a client-server architecture today, such as HTTP and email.

A client-server architecture has the advantage of centralizing access to data, so there won't be multiple potentially out-of-sync copies of the data. Data synchronization is a common problem with distributed systems in general. Data can be processed across multiple nodes, and that processing takes time. If data is changed during the time of processing in one node, but remains the same on another node, then data can be out of sync. The client-server architecture with its central access to data maintains what data to use and manages any synchronization issues.

With well-known protocols, a client-server architecture (Figure 5-10) can have a diverse set of clients that do not need to be implemented in the same programming language or even in the same operating system.

A microservice architecture is a modern variation of the client-server architecture with a client connecting to one or more (micro-, or smaller) services that provide a single capability, or a small set of related capabilities. A microservice has a smaller API and usually less code. Both of these features make individual microservices easier to maintain and secure. However, as the number of microservices grows, coordinating the microservices can become overly complex.

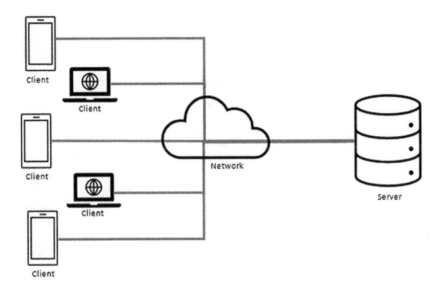

Figure 5-10. *Client-Server Architecture*

Peer to Peer

A peer-to-peer architecture (Figure 5-11) has two or more homogenous nodes in the network that can act as both client and server. This architecture is commonly used for distributed computing where each node does a portion of the computation on a portion of the data. It is also used for file sharing where each node shares distributing part of the files, which is then reassembled at the requesting node.

A peer-to-peer architecture is advantageous when centralized access is not needed, and portions of the work can be done independently. One of the challenges of a peer-to-peer architecture is discovering the peers. Multicast DNS or mDNS is one solution to this challenge. Using mDNS, a peer will send DNS information as a multicast UDP datagram on a network to advertise its presence. Other peers will receive this message to discover a peer. This only works on a single subnet. An alternative approach to discovery is that each peer will register with a central node and ask the central node about the other peers.

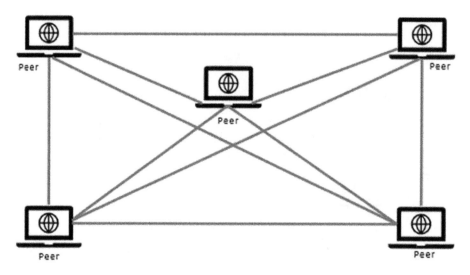

Figure 5-11. *A Peer-to-Peer Architecture*

N-Tiered

An N-tiered architecture (Figure 5-12) is when multiple nodes in the network have specific roles as part of the total solution. One of the most common N-tiered architectures is the three-tiered Model-View-Controller (MVC). The Model service provides the data for a particular model that the View service presents to the user. The Controller service operates on the model and transforms the data as defined by the business logic. This separation of concerns in the architecture provides the advantage of a flexible architecture that holds even when the underlying implementation changes. Model-View-View-Model (MVVM) and Model-View-Presentation (MVP) are other N-tiered architectures you may encounter.

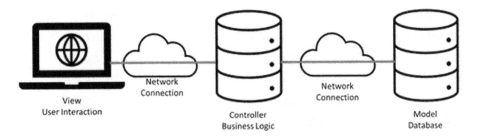

Figure 5-12. *An N-Tiered Architecture*

Distributed System Examples

File transfer (FTP) and the World Wide Web (HTTP) are two examples of distributed systems that we can look into at a detailed level.

FTP

FTP is one of the oldest protocols on the Internet. FTP is implemented with a client-server architecture and is considered a stateful protocol in that the server maintains the state of the connection with the client.

Let's examine what happens when a user wants to download a file from an FTP server (Figure 5-13). First, the user will start the FTP client on their host machine specifying the FTP server by hostname, for instance, ftp.example.com. The FTP client will first resolve the hostname to an IP address via DNS. Once the client has the IP address for ftp.example.com, for instance, 143.11.38.34, the FTP client can create a TCP/IP packet with 143.11.38.34 as the destination and port 21 to designate FTP. This packet gets sent and is received by the first router, which then forwards to the next router and so on until it gets to 143.11.38.34. The FTP server will set up a session for that client and then send a response packet, which will be routed back to the client host. Once the packet is received by the client, it is decoded, and the user is presented with connection information. The user can then log into the FTP server by entering a username and password.

The username is sent to the FTP server as one packet, which the FTP server associates with the session, and the password is sent in clear text as a separate packet to the FTP server. Once the FTP server has both the username and password, the user is authenticated. Now the user can send one or more commands to the FTP server. For the List command, the FTP server will respond with a listing of the files available for download. From here the user can send a Get command to get a specific file. This will open a separate connection to the FTP server on port 22 to receive the requested file. Finally, the user will send the Logout command to terminate the connection. When this packet is received by the FTP server, it "forgets" all of the information for this connection session and sends a connection terminated response back to the FTP client.

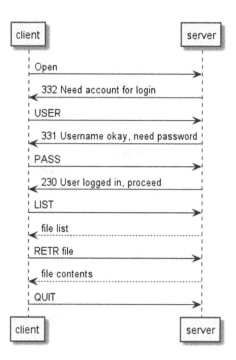

Figure 5-13. *FTP Login and File Transfer Sequence*

The World Wide Web

The modern World Wide Web is a collection of technologies that deliver a variety of services from video and music to banking and retail. One key technology that makes the modern Web so successful is SSL, the Secure Sockets Layer. SSL provides a method using asynchronous keys to encrypt the HTTP payload of a TCP/IP packet. This includes the HTTP headers and body.

For the purpose of simplifying this discussion, we will focus on nonencrypted HTTP (Hypertext Transfer Protocol) in comparison to FTP.

Like FTP, HTTP is a client-server architecture primarily for transferring files. Unlike FTP, HTTP is a stateless protocol, meaning the server does not keep any state about the client. This means HTTP needs to provide all connection information in each packet.

The World Wide Web uses the Uniform Resource Locator (URL) scheme to describe resources on the Web. This scheme defines the protocol, domain hostname or IP address, port, and path to the file. This scheme looks like this with each item in brackets indicating a parameter to specify: `<protocol>://<hostname>:<port>/path/to/file`. The protocol we will use for our example will be HTTP. FTP and HTTPS are two other protocols that can be addressed with an URL. HTTPS for HTTP secure is used to address HTTP through the Secure Sockets Layer and FTP for File Transfer Protocol. For our example, we will use the URL `http://example.com:80/index.html`. This example has HTTP as the protocol, example.com as the hostname, and port 80, which is the default port for HTTP, as the port number. Because we are using the default number for HTTP, we can exclude the port number from the URL.

The user opens a browser and enters the URL into the location field. The browser will decode the URL into its component parts. Just like the FTP client, the first thing the browser will do is resolve the hostname to an IP address. It will then create a TCP/IP packet with the IP address associated with example.com and port number equal to 80, the default port for HTTP. Included in this packet is the HTTP command Get and the requested path. Like all TCP/IP packets, this will be forwarded from router to router until it reaches the server. Here is where HTTP is significantly different than FTP. When the HTTP server receives this packet, it will build a response packet including the contents of the file at the path, in our case index.html. The server will send this response packet back to the client and forget everything about that transaction (it won't keep state). When the response packet is received by the browser, the data content is parsed and rendered in your browser window. Table 5-2 lists the HTTP response code sent back to the client.

Table 5-2. *HTTP Response Codes*

Class	Code text	Code	Meaning
Success	OK	200	Request successfully fulfilled.
Success	Created	201	Used by the Post method to indicate newly created document.
Success	Accepted	202	Request has been accepted for processing, but is not yet processed.
Success	Partial Information	203	Not the definitive document requested but metainformation.
Success	No Response	204	Server received the request but does not send any information back.
Redirection	Moved	301	Requested document has permanently moved to a new URL. Header will contain a new URL.
Redirection	Found	302	Requested document has a different URL, but this is a valid URL.

(continued)

Table 5-2. (*continued*)

Class	Code text	Code	Meaning
Redirection	Method	303	Requested document not available with this method.
Redirection	Not Modified	304	Requested document has not changed; the client should use the cache.
Client Errors	Bad Request	400	Request had bad syntax or is impossible to fulfill.
Client Errors	Unauthorized	401	Request does not have a suitable Authorization header.
Client Errors	Payment Required	402	The request requires a ChargeTo header information.
Client Errors	Forbidden	403	Request is forbidden; there is no suitable Authorization header.
Client Errors	Not Found	404	The server has not found anything matching the URL.
Server Error	Internal Error	500	The server encountered an error.
Server Error	Not Implemented	501	The server has not implemented the facility to fulfill the request.
Server Error	Service Temporarily Overloaded	502	The server cannot fulfill this request do to load.
Server Error	Gateway Timeout	503	Similar to 500 error, but indicates the server cannot access another server.

While HTTP was originally developed for transferring HTML documents, "web pages," the versatility of a stateless protocol has allowed for a wider variety of applications to be implemented on top of the World Wide Web. ReST (Resource Stateless Transfer) is a method of creating general-purpose APIs using HTTP. ReST APIs will typically transfer documents that contain data. JavaScript Object Notation or JSON and the Extensible Markup Language (XML) are two common formats that are used for these data-rich documents. The data is sent to a client that may or may not be a browser.

Case Study: Web Application

As a case study, we will build a simple web application. This application will provide a browser-based form to request a user-specified number of files to recommend to the user and then allow the user to select one of those files to download from the back end.

System Architecture

This system will have three main components (Figure 5-14). On the front end will be a browser form that provides the user input. In the middle will be the HTTP ReST server that receives the requests from the front end. Finally, we have the data source that the server will use to choose files from.

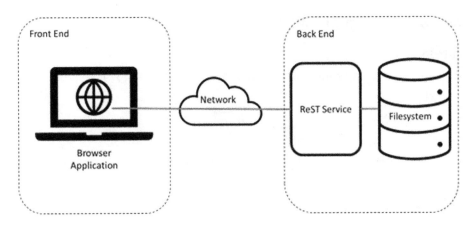

Figure 5-14. *Web Application Three-Tiered Architecture*

As part of the architecture for a ReST service, it will be important to define the resources that will be available before implementation. We will define the first resource as filelist with a URL of http://example.com/filelist/<count>. Each file that is available will also have a URL that will be http://example.com/files/<filename>, and finally the HTML content for the front end will be served from http://example.com/app.html.

HTML, CSS, and JavaScript

Before we dive into this solution, let's do a brief intro on HTML and some related topics. HTML stands for HyperText Markup Language and was the original intended format to be sent by HTTP. HTML provides a way of marking up a document into different sections using tags such as <head>, <body>, <script>, <div> for division, the paragraph tag <p>, and many others, as shown in Listing 5-1. The sections are separated by a beginning tag <body> and an ending tag </body>. Tags can and do contain other tags.

Listing 5-1. Simple HTML Example

```
<html>
    <header><title>Network Example Client</title></header>
    <body>
        <div>
            <p>Hello Today</p>
        </div>
    </body>
</html>
```

Cascading Style Sheets or CSS is a method of providing styling information to the sections or tags of the documents. The style can be applied directly in the HTML document using a <style> tag or defined in a separate document and linked to the HTML document.

JavaScript is a programming language that is embedded in most web browsers and provides a programmatic access to the contents of the HTML document and the ability to alter the contents of the HTML document in the browser's memory. Similar to CSS, JavaScript code can be embedded in the HTML document using a <script> tag or defined in a separate document and linked to the HTML document. JSON is the native object definition syntax for JavaScript, allowing JavaScript code to easily read and manipulate JSON documents.

Front End

For the front end (Listing 5-2), we could use an HTML form, but we would like to get a little more dynamic and be able to update the view of the form without making additional requests to the app.html. The app.html will include a form to ask the user how many files they would like to see as options. JavaScript will connect, get the user input, and then form an HTTP request packet with the URL to the filelist route that includes the number of files to be provided as options. An HTTP request will be sent via the browser to the back-end server. The server will send back a response containing JSON-formatted data that includes the files that the back end selected for options and the URLs for each file in the back end. The front end will then interpret this JSON data and update the form in the browser to show the file options to the user. Then the user will select one of the options, after which the front-end client will build an HTTP request to get the selected file. The back end will then respond with the contents for the file to the front end.

Listing 5-2. HTML and JavaScript for a Client

```
<html>
    <header><title>Network Example Client</title>
        <script >
            function load(){
                var xhttp = new XMLHttpRequest();
                var count = document.getElementById("count").value
                xhttp.onreadystatechange = function() {
                    if (this.readyState == 4 && this.status == 200) {
                        suggestions(this)
                    }
                };
                xhttp.open("GET", "filelist/"+count, true);
                xhttp.send();
            }
            function suggestions(resp) {
                var item_list = JSON.parse(resp.responseText);
                var suggest_html = "<ul>"
                item_list.forEach(element => {
                    suggest_html = suggest_html+'<li><a href="'
+element[1]+'">'+element[0]+"</a></li>"

                });
```

```
                    suggest_html+="</ul>"
                    document.getElementById("list").innerHTML =
                    suggest_html;
                }
        </script>
    </header>
        <body>
        <H1>Network Demo</H1>
        <div>
            <input id="count" value=5>
            <button onclick=load()>Select</button>
        </div>
        <div id="list">
            <p>Select a Random list books</p>
        </div>
        </body>
</html>
```

Back End

The back end (Listing 5-3) will be a ReST service running on a system
with a set of files on a disk. The first request the back end expects to get is
a request for the front-end application at the route app.html. This is not
required to be the first request because the back-end server is stateless.
When it gets the request for app.html, the back end will return the HTML
file to the browser, which the browser will render. Then the back end is
ready to receive the next request. The next request could be a request for
a number of files, for instance, to the route "filelist/3." With this request,
the back end will parse the value 3 from the path and use that in a pseudorandom selection of three of the files from the disk. The back end will
then encode a JSON object containing the name and URL for each of the

files and respond back to the front end. At this point, the back end will be ready to receive another request. The next request we might expect from the front end is a request for one of the files presented in the last response. Here the back end will read the file from the disk and create a response containing the contents of the file to send to the front end.

Listing 5-3. Python Flask Code for Serving the Back End

```python
@routes.get('/filelist/{count}')
async def filelist(request):
    count = int(request.match_info.get("count",0))
    filelist = list(get_example(EXAMPLES, count))
    headers = {"Cache-Control": "no-cache"}
    return web.json_response(filelist, headers=headers)

@routes.get("/")
async def index(request):
    index = pathlib.Path(pathlib.Path(__file__).parent,
    "index.html")
    resp_text = index.read_text()
    return web.Response(text=resp_text, content_type="text/html")
```

Summary

In this chapter, we have covered a wide range of topics related to distributed systems and networks. We started with the history and evolution of the networking protocols that have brought us to the modern Internet. Next, we looked into the IPs that enable networks to work, such as TCP and UDP. Building on this, we examined specific protocols on top of UDP such as DNS and DHCP that help define the networks. And then we looked at the capabilities provided by TCP, such as FTP. After that we saw some common architectures for distributed systems including client-server and peer-to-peer. Finally, we pulled all this knowledge together to create a simple client-server application using HTTP and related technologies, HTML and JavaScript.

References and Further Reading

- James Kurose and Keith Ross. *Computer Networking: A Top-Down Approach, Seventh Edition.* Pearson, 2016

- W. Richard Stevens, Bill Fenner, and Andrew M. Rudoff. *Unix Network Programming, Volume 1: The Sockets Networking API, Third Edition.* Addison-Wesley Professional, 2004

- Janet Abbate. *Inventing the Internet.* MIT Press, 1999

CHAPTER 6

Computer Security

Computer security is an extremely broad field spanning across multiple domains, ranging from the security of user data to the physical safety of the user. On a commercial robot, for instance, computer security is used to protect sensors and actuators whose malicious use can have a devastating impact on human life. Some examples of critical computer systems that could be compromised, if they have security issues, are healthcare systems, missile defense systems, and aviation systems, to name a few. Security spans from hardware and software to the social behavior of the users of the computer. In computer security, most things are not unconditionally secure; in general, they are only computationally secure. In other words, most security primitives are secure only under a given set of assumptions about the adversary. As computers are evolving, the amount of computation resources available to an adversary is increasing exponentially, year over year. As a result, security mechanisms must be upgraded to ensure the same level of security over time. Colloquially, it is a cat-and-mouse game where the defender must stay one step ahead of the adversary. The complex topic of physical safety is out of scope for this book. In this chapter, we will focus on data security, including types of security, adversary models, and mechanisms to secure data at rest (in storage) and data in transit between computer systems.

Privacy is another field that is always strongly associated with security. The fundamental security mechanisms used to protect data are the same mechanisms used to protect privacy. Privacy is associated with one or more users and pertains to the confidentiality of Personally Identifiable Information (PII). With the advent of targeted online advertisements, privacy of users comes under scrutiny as both users and governments are worried about the data collection companies knowing too much about users and being able to predict their next actions. Sometimes, users voluntarily share their personal data in exchange for a free service; and in other cases, hidden software collects data from cameras, computers, and other devices used by the consumer without the explicit approval of the user. This is an evolving field with new primitives like differential privacy being developed in order to balance economic and human needs.

Access Control

Like any other advanced field, computer security has its own jargon. In this section, we demystify common terms that are used by media, industry, and security experts to express ideas around security. As security is all about protecting data, there are certain fundamental security properties of data that need exposition. Data can have the following security properties: Read, Write, and Execute. Data is readable for an actor if the actor can read the data without being blocked by any agent in the system. The data is writable if the actor can write the data in the system without being blocked by any other agent. Finally, the data is executable if an actor can point an agent to execute the commands. An astute reader will notice that the properties of data are from the perspective of an actor. In other words, same piece of data that is readable for one actor may be only writable for another or executable for yet another actor, or a combination of these properties for the same piece of data may be valid for another actor. In a computer system, these properties are specified by software and enforced by hardware. This is also called as *access control* of data and is enforced by a *trusted* agent in the system. The trusted agent will have all access to the data and will grant selective access to other agents and actors. The agents and actors in a computer system span both hardware and software.

In many cases, it is not possible to use access control for enforcing the properties of data. In those scenarios, we need to use cryptography. Cryptography is the art and science of protection of data in the presence of adversaries. This is a vast field of study, and in this chapter, we will talk about the fundamental properties of data that can be enforced using cryptography. The cryptographic properties are similar to the access control properties that can be enforced, but the mechanisms of the enforcement are vastly different. In addition, in certain scenarios, access control can be enforced, while in other scenarios, like sending data over an untrusted channel, cryptographic mechanisms must be used. It is important to point out here that most of the modern cryptographic algorithms and protocols are only secure under assumptions of compute limitations of an adversary. An adversary with unlimited compute capability can bypass most of the cryptographic mechanisms being used today. We introduce common cryptographic and security properties in the rest of this section.

Confidentiality

Confidentiality of data covers if the data is secret or not. It is clearly a corollary to the Read property explained in the preceding under access control. If an actor can read a data, it is not confidential to the actor. If the actor cannot read it, it is confidential to the actor. There is a long list of encryption algorithms that are used to encrypt data to ensure its confidentiality. Unencrypted data, called *plaintext*, is sent through an encryption algorithm to generate a ciphertext. A key is used for encryption. As shown in Figure 6-1, in a symmetric encryption algorithm, the same key is also used for decryption, the process of generating the plaintext from ciphertext. Any actor that has the key has the read access to this data since it can *decrypt* the ciphertext and read the plaintext. Since the same key is used for encryption and decryption, this mechanism is called Symmetric Encryption. In the United States, there is a body called the National Institute of Standards and Technology (NIST) that standardizes encryption algorithms that are used by most of the industry. Currently, the strongest encryption algorithm standardized and recommended by NIST is Advanced Encryption Standard (AES).

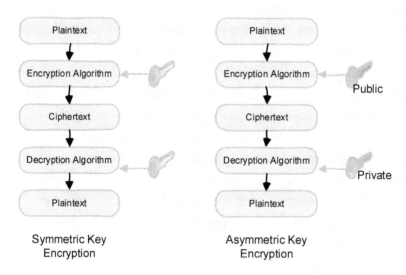

Figure 6-1. *Symmetric and Asymmetric Encryption*

AES succeeds DES (Data Encryption Standard) and 3DES and is considered much more secure than its predecessors. Most cryptographic libraries provide APIs (application programming interfaces) for AES encryption; and most general-purpose processors from Intel, Apple, AMD (Advanced Micro Devices), and ARM support instructions for acceleration of AES encryption and decryption.

Integrity

Integrity of data implies whether the data has been modified or not. It is a corollary to the Write property explained in the preceding under access control. If an actor can write a data, the integrity of the data is controlled by the actor. To ensure the integrity of data, data may be encrypted using a symmetric algorithm, and the same ciphertext will give the same plaintext using the same key. The problem we have is what if the adversary changes the ciphertext; on subsequent decryption of the modified ciphertext, the plaintext will be different from the original plaintext, which is clearly not desirable. The concept of hashing was introduced to solve this problem. Hashing is the process of mapping an arbitrary-length data blob to a fixed-size data blob called hash. The hashing algorithms are one-way functions such that given a hash value, it is computationally infeasible (or extremely hard) to find another data blob that would compress to the same hash value. In addition, a given data blob will always hash to the same hash value as long as the same algorithm is used. In order to ensure the integrity of the data blob, the hash value is protected from the adversary by either storing it separately from the data blob or encrypting it. If the adversary modifies the data blob, the hash value will change, and the hash of the modified data blob will not match the original hash value. Also, as mentioned in the preceding, it is computationally infeasible to find two blobs that will map to the same hash.

SHA-3 and SHA-512 are common hash functions used in cryptography. SHA-512 and SHA-3 can support a maximum of 512 bits of hash. In other words, any large blob can be hashed to 512 bits of hash. An astute reader will note that multiple large blobs can be hashed to a set of 512 bits. As a result, the data-to-hash relationship is two way; however, it is considered extremely hard (computationally intensive) to find a *new plaintext* that will hash to the same hash. In other words, if H(x) =Y, it is highly computationally intensive to find x' such that H(x') =Y.

Availability

Availability of data points to the physical presence of the data. It implies if the data is available to the actor to read, write, or execute. In other words, if an actor has access to the data but the data is deleted from its location in storage or memory or an adversary prevents a legitimate actor from accessing the data to which the actor has permissions, the data is considered to be no longer *available*. Cryptography generally does not help with availability as the operating system controls deletion of data. Availability is ensured by restricting access of an adversary to the data.

Symmetric Key Cryptography

The preceding cryptographic and access control mechanisms work very well within a single system. However, the security problems become much more complex when multiple systems on the network are involved and the network channel is untrusted. If we have multiple systems on the network, we need protocols to ensure that a network adversary cannot interfere with the integrity of the data being transferred on the network. If Alice's computer wants to send a confidential letter to Bob's computer, Mallory, who has access to the network channel, should not be able read or write the messages between Bob and Alice. In addition, we want to ensure that Mallory should not be able to *replay* the messages from Alice to Bob. For example, if Alice wants to ask Bob to withdraw 20 dollars from the bank, Mallory should not be able to capture the message and replay it to Bob and make Bob withdraw 20 dollars multiple times, something which Alice never intended to do. The same mechanisms for encryption and hashing work in this scenario, but we get into a problem of sharing the keys between Alice and Bob so that Bob could decrypt the message.

Symmetric encryption algorithms become problematic in network communication because there needs to be a secure way for the two sides to have the same key. In the preceding example, if Alice needs to encrypt and Bob needs to decrypt, they both must have the same key. In the absence of fast and secure communication channels, there is no way to send the key such that Mallory cannot get it. This is where *asymmetric key* cryptography comes in.

Asymmetric Key Cryptography

Asymmetric key cryptography, as shown in Figure 6-1, is a set of algorithms enabling cryptographic operation with one key and its reversal with another key. For example, a data blob can be encrypted with a public key PuKey1 and decrypted with another private key PrKey1. As a result, Alice and Bob can agree on a PuKey1 and a PrKey1 allowing Alice to send messages encrypted with PrKey1 and letting Bob decrypt the messages with PuKey1. Alice's key is called the private key, and Bob's key is called the public key. The mechanism used by Alice and Bob is called the key establishment protocol. There are multiple key establishment protocols being used in the industry including RSA based on its authors Rivest-Shamir-Adelman, DHKP (Diffie-Hellman Key Establishment Protocol), and ECC (Elliptic Curve Cryptography). All the protocols are based on a mathematical algorithm like discrete logarithms, factorization of prime numbers, and so on with a common theme that it is easy to compute the results in one way and almost impossible (without the knowledge of the keys) to reverse this computation. These key establishment protocols are computationally expensive; hence, they are not used to encrypt a lot of data. Instead, they are used to establish a shared symmetric key between the two parties, and the symmetric key is then used to encrypt/decrypt the data on the channel. This provides the best security while minimizing the overhead that comes with such security solutions.

Digital Signatures

Cryptography provides us a way of doing digital signatures, exactly like we sign a checkbook from our bank. When we sign a checkbook, the bank can verify our signature, we cannot deny signing it, and we cannot reuse a check once the money has been withdrawn and cannot repudiate that we signed the check. Digital signatures provide all these properties for digital documents. A digital signature is done by hashing a document and then encrypting the hash with a private key. Any entity (like a bank) that has the public key can verify that the document is signed by the owner of the private key. The bank saves the signed copy with a check number such that the owner or some intermediary cannot reuse the signed document again. One important thing to note is that digital signatures do not provide confidentiality but only provide nonrepudiation and integrity. The protocols built on digital signatures provide protection against replay attacks. In many countries including the United States, European Union countries, and India, digital signatures are also legally admissible in court.

Digital Certificates

Any entity with a computer can generate a public/private key pair. How do we know that this public/private key belongs to Alice or Bob? Well, we need someone to tell us that the public/private key belongs to Alice or Bob. This is where the certificate authority comes into play. A certificate authority is a well-known agency like the driver license office or the government that issues passports. Everybody knows the driver license office and trusts them. This concept is taken to the digital world where well-known companies sign up to become certificate authorities (CAs). They are trusted by the rest of us because these companies are in the business of issuing certificates and any wrong endorsement from them significantly hurts their credibility and their business. In this scenario, the CA issues a certificate that tells everybody the hash of the public key of Alice or Bob. This way whenever Alice or Bob signs anything with their private key, any verifier can verify the signature and also check whether the key belonged to Alice or Bob.

The most common certificates used in the industry are X.509 certificates. These certificates have the details of the subject and the issuer and the public key of the subject. They are signed with the private key of the issuer (CA).

Certificate Chains

Since one CA cannot sign certificates for everyone, the certificate signing architectures are generally distributed, where one or more CAs form a central ring and they issue certificates to the large corporations in the outer ring. Large corporations issue certificates to their people, products, and devices, essentially forming a certificate chain rooted in the innermost circle, the CA itself. These certificate chains are also called chains of trust where the root certificate is the trusted certificate and all the child certificates derive trust from the root certificate.

Salts and Nonces

Salts are random bits of data generated using a random number generator. Salts are commonly used as an input to a hashing or an encryption algorithm such that the output of the algorithm is randomized. They are commonly used in password systems where passwords are stored to protect them from pre-computation or dictionary attacks. For example, a password X= "password" can be hashed using a function F(X)=Y. If an adversary knows the length of the password and that it is made from the English alphabet, the adversary can pre-compute a dictionary of all permutations of eight English alphabet letters. As a result, when it sees the hash, all it needs is to look for the corresponding hash in its dictionary and it can find the password string. However, if we generate a 64-bit random number R and concatenate it with the password such that F(X||R) = Y, the adversary will have to generate 2^{64} = 18,446,744,073,709,551,616 (20 digits) dictionaries in order to find the password.

Nonces are also random bits of data generated using a random number generator and used as an input to various cryptographic algorithms. Nonces are not a secret from an adversary and commonly not repeated. In network protocols, nonces are used for ensuring the order of the packets and protecting from an adversary that tries to benefit by reordering the packets.

Random Numbers

Random numbers are a foundational element of cryptography and computer security. They are used for generating keys, nonces, and salts. A salt is a random bit. Sometimes, they are used to seed counters used in symmetric encryption algorithms. Intuitively simple, true random numbers are extremely hard to generate in a computer system because of lack of entropy (randomness) in computer hardware and software algorithms. As a result, special-purpose primitives are built in the computer systems to provide this entropy. There are really three kinds of random numbers. First, *True Random Numbers (TRNs)* are numbers generated from a physical phenomenon like a flip of a coin. They are exceedingly difficult to emulate with deterministic algorithms on computers. The second kind of random numbers are *pseudorandom numbers*. Here, a seed is created from randomness of the computer, using an entropy source like user inputs, heat of the system, speed of the fan, and so on; and this random value is used as a seed to generate pseudorandom numbers. Given the seed and the algorithm, the next number can be predicted, hence the name pseudorandom. *Cryptographically secure random numbers* are the third class of random numbers commonly used in cryptography. These provide forward secrecy (knowing a number from the series will not divulge any previous numbers in the series) and break-in recovery (knowing a number from the series will not divulge future numbers).

Security in Client Computing Systems

In the previous section, we read about the fundamental primitives for security of any system. The two fundamental primitives we read about are cryptographic mechanisms and access control. In most security solutions, one of these two mechanisms is used for protecting any asset. In the next section, we look at some of the contemporary technologies that the industry has developed in order to provide secure experiences in client computing. We have talked about the fundamental principles and primitives used for security and cryptography in the previous section. In the next few sections, let us discuss how these primitives are used in modern-day compute clients, servers, and the network. Modern-day clients (including desktops, laptops, phones), networks (including the Internet), and servers (IT [information technology] servers, external servers on the Internet, cloud servers) all attempt to work together to provide seamless security to the user. Client systems not only depend on the local platform mechanisms for security, but they also depend on servers in the cloud to configure and manage security locally. The client security comprises primitives for protecting data at rest, data in motion, and data in use and intersects with network security wherever data in motion must be protected.

Malware, the Bad Apples of Software

In an industry where millions of lines of code are written per day, there are thousands of hidden defects in said code. In the software parlance, these defects are called bugs. These bugs can be further classified into two main categories. The first category consists of nonsecurity bugs where the code is doing something other than what the programmer intended it to do. These bugs may impact the user experience, functionality, safety, and/or the performance of the system. The second kind of bugs are more interesting from a security perspective. These bugs, named *vulnerabilities*, are opportunities for an adversary to exploit the system to steal and abuse user data and/or illegitimately change the behavior and/or characteristics of the system. Malicious software that exploits these vulnerabilities is called malware. The malware that exploits these vulnerabilities is further classified into virus, worm, trojan, and so on based on the mechanisms used by the malware, its goals, and the impact it has on the user's system. Skoudis et al. supply a good overview of the classification of all kinds of malware found in the wild in their book. In this chapter, we will abstract out the types of malware and focus on malware in general.

Malware is written by a myriad of actors, from so-called script kiddies who cobble together scripts to exploit a vulnerability to organized crime houses, sometimes funded by state agencies to indulge in cyber warfare. There is also an open market for malware called Darknet. Most malware will use multiple vulnerabilities to attack the system and follows the BORE (Break Once, Run Everywhere) model. This provides the malware writer motivation to devote resources to write the malware and then be able to use it repeatedly on a large number of machines till the vulnerability is fixed. Even when the vulnerability patches (software updates) are released by the original software vendor, it can take a long time (sometimes years) for these patches to reach all the end systems. Although the delivery mechanisms have become more efficient in the vertically integrated ecosystems like some phones, they are far from perfect.

Malware is extremely hard to detect because it looks like benign software to the untrained eye. However, the anti-malware industry has figured out a way to detect *known* malware with the help of antivirus (AV) scanners. The anti-malware industry employs security researchers to characterize a malware and generate a fingerprint for it. This fingerprint, called the *signature* (not to be confused with a cryptographic signature), is then fed into the antivirus scanners running on the computers. The antivirus scanner then searches for the known signatures in the software stored and executing on the platform. If a signature matches, it alerts the user and/or deletes the malware from the system. This search-based mechanism has served the industry well since 1988 when the *Morris Worm* was found in the field. However, these signatures are very fragile such that changing one bit in the malware code can change this signature and provide a way for the malware to bypass the scrutiny of the antivirus running on the system. As the number of viruses is increasing and the number of corresponding signatures is rising to the order of millions, the antivirus companies are struggling in this battle with malware writers. Malware authors can now write self-modifying malware, also called homomorphic malware. The enormous number of signatures does not only consume heavy compute resources, but they are also easy to circumvent due to the ability of the malware to self-modify. Fortunately, the advent of artificial intelligence (AI) and neural networks has given us a new set of tools against malware. In the AI-based approach, the antivirus (AV) companies extract attributes of the malware and create a deep learning model from those attributes. Some examples of these attributes include function names in the malware, IP (Internet Protocol) addresses used, variable names, source of malware used, and so on. Since malware writers tend to reuse code, even modified malware has remnants of its parents. A new malware when passed through the inference engine is likely to get detected as malware even if some bits have been modified from the parent.

Security of Data at Rest

Most user data on clients is stored on either a flash-based SSD (solid-state drive) or a magnetic disk. This data is the easiest to steal for an adversary. The adversary can steal the device, pull out the hard disk or SSD, connect it to another system, and read all the data. The industry has been worried about this physical attack for a long time; as a result, full-disk encryption solutions have been developed to fend off such attacks. All user data stored on the disk is encrypted, and the key is bound to the user and the device such that the data can only be decrypted when the user logs into the same device. This prevents an adversary from using another device or another user login to illegitimately access the data. Most modern operating systems have disk encryption built in them including Windows, Chrome OS (operating system), iOS, Android, and macOS. Disk encryption provides the user an assurance that their data is secured even if the device is lost or stolen.

Security of Data in Use

Protecting data at runtime is harder due to the fast-evolving nature of malware that tries to steal data and/or alter execution paths at runtime. Most general-purpose compute devices provide hardware mechanisms for software isolation like

- Process isolation

- Separation of privileged code from nonprivileged code

- Execute-disable bits – make modifiable memory as non-executable

- Mechanisms to protect the stacks – protection against stack overflows

- Protections against Return-Oriented Programming attacks (ROP attacks)

Client systems even go further to provide trusted execution environments (TEEs) to run algorithms at higher-privilege levels. Some examples of these TEEs are the secure virtual machines running on top of VMMs (Virtual Machine Monitors) and security controllers in the platform. They all run code at high-privilege levels where most malware finds it hard to attack them. Although the industry has been churning out increasingly capable defense mechanisms, the bad guys have not stopped. As a result, we are likely to see increased progress in mechanisms for protecting runtime environments on client platforms in the coming years.

In 2018, some researchers from the Google Zero project found a way to exploit branch prediction in CPUs (central processing units) to do a privilege escalation attack. The most prominent attacks on branch prediction have been Spectre and Meltdown. This led to a flurry of security fix patches from silicon and operating system vendors, impacting millions of systems. This was an attack that was thought to be too computationally intensive to run, but with improved CPU performance on modern systems, it is now extremely feasible. This was a stark reminder for the industry that nothing is really absolutely secure. Even if something has stood up to the test of time for decades, it does not mean it is completely secure.

Application vs. Kernel vs. Drivers

Most general-purpose operating systems are structured in a similar way such that the operating system (or the kernel) manages the hardware and runs at a higher privilege than the applications. General-purpose computing processors provide hardware mechanisms for the operating systems to protect their own execution and I/O (input/output) from applications. Applications run at user privilege, a lower privilege level than the OS itself. In addition, we try to make sure that for any code that runs on the platform, its provenance or origin is known before it executes. As a result, most applications are signed by their owners and verified by the operating system on which they execute. These signatures are cryptographic signatures that have a certificate chain rooted in a well-known CA that is used to identify their owners. This provides multiple security benefits: (a) It makes sure that the owner of the application does not introduce a malware in the application, since it can be traced back to them. (b) It deters malware writers since they must get a certificate in order to sign the malicious application.

I/O hardware generally has an associated piece of code that is used to manage the hardware. This piece of code, called the driver, typically runs in a privileged mode under the OS. Drivers decouple the I/O from the rest of the operating system, provide a granular way to manage the I/O including updates, and are isolated from the applications. However, since these drivers live in the privileged domain, they must be protected, and the kernel must be protected from them. To harden them, these drivers are signed and verified by the OS like other applications. Every general-purpose operating system provides a mechanism of signing and verifying drivers.

User Authentication and Authorization

Another way of protecting user data is to provide strong authentication for the user and the actors trying to access the data. Identifying and verifying the identity of the user is named as user authentication. Once the user is authenticated, it is granted access to certain resources. This grant is called authorization. User authentication has significantly evolved in the industry, from user passwords that by themselves are inherently unsecure to biometric authentication that may use face and/or fingerprinting to other multifactor techniques, such as texting passcodes. Biometrics and multifactor techniques have significantly enhanced the security and experience of authentication. Multifactor authentication requires the user to prove who they are via two or more of the following criteria: something they have (e.g., a phone that can be texted a passcode), something they know (e.g., a password), and/or something they are (e.g., a fingerprint or their face). The fundamental problems with passwords are that as the length and complexity requirements of passwords increased, it became harder for the users to remember them. As a result, users started using the same passwords for different systems, like websites. To address such password reuse, these sites add "salt" and then hash these passwords and save the resulting hash to disk. With this scheme, if an adversary compromises a server, it would be able to see only the hashed passwords. It can still do an offline dictionary attack (copy the file to its local storage and try to crack it) on the salted password, but this is a much harder problem than cracking unsalted passwords. If the hacker can discover the password, they can potentially compromise many of that user's accounts over many websites where the user was using the same password. This was clearly an undesirable situation.

It used to be that industry used to shy away from biometric authentication because of the fundamental concerns around non-replaceability of biometric data for a given user. That has changed now, and the industry is rallying behind biometric authentication although sending biometric data over the network is still frowned upon. User authentication is done at multiple levels, from a user login into the OS to a user login into a website. The current state of the art in user authentication is FIDO (Fast Identity Online), which turns the user authentication around. A user generates a private-public key pair and sends the public key to the server. The private key is protected using a pin or biometric authentication on the client, and the public key is saved at the server. Every unique website has a different public-private key pair, so a compromise of the public key at the server does not compromise the user account, since the adversary cannot do much with the public key without possessing the private key.

Trusted Execution Environments and Virtual Machines

Traditionally software running on mainstream computers has been classified into user applications (like browsers, file explorers, etc.) and operating system that hosts these applications. The operating system is the supervisor that manages all the hardware resources on the platform and selectively grants them to the applications. Most people are familiar with Windows, Chrome OS, and macOS. Since the operating system runs at a higher-privilege level, by the virtue of managing resources, it also enforces access control. The applications run at a lower privilege level from the operating system, thereby insulating the operating system from the applications. As the threat landscape has evolved, it turns out that operating system–level access control is no longer sufficient. There is a trend to run applications in an environment that is more secure than the operating system itself. These are not traditional applications like Notepad but purpose-built applications for security, like a user login service. These specialized environments, isolated from the operating system, are called trusted execution environments (TEEs). These are highly secure environments running extra secure applications. Trusted execution environments may run on a separate controller as a peer to the host operating system, albeit with higher privileges than the host operating system. The alternative is to have TEEs run on the same controller as the host operating system in a time-sliced fashion and with higher privileges. Virtual Machine Monitors (VMMs) are used to achieve the latter, while security controllers are used to achieve the former. These TEEs are protected from the operating system and user applications and provide higher security than the operating system itself.

Traditionally one platform could run one operating system, but it turned out that one operating system was not able to consume all the resources of the platform. Virtualization was then invented to solve the problem of running multiple operating systems. Virtualized systems run virtual machines that are containers for operating systems. All the virtual machines on the OS are managed by another layer of software called a Virtual Machine Monitor (VMM). Since the VMM can isolate the VMs from each other, VMs have become one way of instantiating a TEE. VM-based TEEs are commonly used in commercial OSs in the market.

Secure Boot

Secure boot is the process of loading and executing mutable code after verifying the first mutable code by hardware. Mutable code is code that can be modified (before execution) in non-volatile storage like a disk or a solid-state drive. Subsequent mutable code is verified by the previously verified mutable code, thereby forming a chain. It is commonly used to protect from malware attacks that modify firmware/software in persistent storage and is a common industry practice now. The main goal of secure boot is to ensure that only the system firmware and OS from a trusted source execute on the client. As explained previously, the OS makes sure that the applications and drivers are signed and sources are verified.

Most commodity hardware provides mechanisms for secure boot. They might either have a non-mutable code embedded in the hardware (in a ROM) or have a security controller that is responsible for verifying the mutable code. Clearly the code for the security controller itself must go through secure boot, and for that non-mutable code is typically stored in the ROM. Figure 6-2 shows a typical scenario of secure boot.

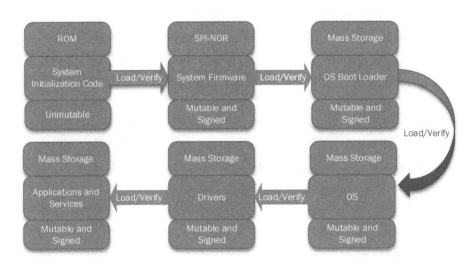

Figure 6-2. *Secure Boot*

The preceding diagram shows a typical secure boot session. In each node in the diagram, the topmost bubble shows where the code is stored, the middle bubble shows what the code is, and the lowermost bubble shows whether the code is mutable and signed. Most client platforms boot from a program stored in read-only memory (ROM). This program is considered unmutable since it is programmed in the memory at the factory and cannot be modified after that. Once this program executes, it loads the next program from persistent storage. The persistent storage can be limited (few megabytes) storage in the form of a SPI-NOR or be a big storage drive sized to the order of terabytes. The program in the persistent storage is considered mutable since the persistent storage can be modified by an adversary. As a result, the ROM program checks the cryptographic signature of the program in memory before executing it. This ensures all the programs that execute are cryptographically verified.

Secure I/O

Human beings interact with the computer using I/O peripherals. The security of the I/O peripherals is of utmost importance. Let us take a common scenario of money transfer; Alice wants to send 100 dollars to Bob, and she fills out a bank form on her favorite browser. Mallory implants a malware in the path from her keyboard to the browser and in the path from the browser to the display. When Alice types Bob, the browser receives the name Mallory. Although the browser wants to display Mallory in the window, the malware makes it display Bob. When Alice clicks Submit, the money gets transferred from Alice's account to Mallory's account. Most operating systems own and manage the I/O channels like keyboard, mouse, display, and so on. However, this makes both the OS and the I/O devices vulnerable to malware in the OS or in the device itself. Connecting the device directly to a TEE (trusted execution environment) protects the TEE and the device from OS malware. This connection can be a logical connection where there is a security protocol between the device and the TEE or a physical connection where the TEE directly manages the physical port connected to the device. Secure storage is also another form of secure I/O where the TEE manages the storage.

Digital Rights Management

Digital Rights Management (DRM) came into prominence with the
Digital Millennium Copyright Act (DMCA). It criminalizes copyright
infringement or attempts to evade protections put in place to control
access to copyright works. More commonly, it is used to protect videos
and music from unlicensed consumption. Most client computing devices
provide mechanisms for the user to be able to access licensed content
while deterring the user from accessing unlicensed content. These security
mechanisms commonly work with the help of a TEE. Typically, the client
first enrolls with a content provider. Once the server has identified and
authenticated with the client, it provides the encrypted content (movie
or music) to the client along with the license. The TEE then decrypts the
content and coordinates with the operating system to play the content on
the selected media device. The hardware and the software on the client
ensure that the licensed user can access the content but cannot copy the
content for redistribution or for use on another device. An astute reader
will notice this is one of the fields in computer security where the owner of
the device itself is not completely trusted with the data present on the user
platform, since the user is not the owner of the movie but only a consumer
of it. From the perspective of the content industry, as they are pouring
billions into new content, they need these DRM mechanisms to protect
their investments.

Communication Security: Security of Data in Motion

Most computers converse over an untrusted channel on the Internet. Even
though corporate and home networks are considered more trustworthy
due to the restricted physical access to the data cables and data signals on
which the data travels, the trend is going toward open networks where the

clients are expected to reduce their trust in the network channels and take appropriate cryptographic and security measures to ensure that the data can travel securely over untrusted networks.

On the network, the security protocols used must ensure the confidentiality, integrity, and/or replay protection of data. There are really no protocols available today that can protect against denial of service in an adversarial network. In other words, if Alice sends a message to Bob and Mallory is sitting on the adversarial network, Mallory can drop the message, and there is nothing Alice or Bob can do about it except Bob informing Alice that he did not receive a certain message and Alice resending it. The following three protocols are commonly used to ensure the security properties of the data on the network.

Transport Layer Security

TLS (Transport Layer Security) is the second generation of the Secure Sockets Layer (SSL) cryptographic protocol that is designed to protect data being sent over an untrusted network. It is commonly used between a web browser running on a client and the server providing the service. The use of TLS has expanded to email servers, chat servers, voice calls, and even media streaming in some cases. TLS provides confidentiality and integrity of the messages using cryptographic asymmetric and symmetric key mechanisms. In common scenarios, web browsers do a bidirectional authentication with the server, that is, the server authenticates the client device and the client authenticates the server.

TLS (Transport Layer Security) and encryption on the Internet in general are seen as a double-edge sword by the government and the regulatory bodies across the world. The same secure conduit that allows users to protect their data from adversaries on the network is also used by malware to send malicious data across the network while avoiding the prying eyes of the government and regulatory agencies. Governments want to be able to monitor the data, and privacy advocates do not want any loopholes in privacy protocols – the debate is ongoing.

Figure 6-3 shows the Open Systems Interconnection (OSI) layers of a network stack. Although data protection applies to all these layers, most security solutions use TLS in the transport layer and IPSec (Internet Protocol Security) in the network layer while resorting to purpose-built protocols in the application layer. The cryptographic primitives used by these protocols remain the same, while the messaging formats and the number of messages in the protocols change. It is also common to see data being encrypted multiple times as it travels down the stack and getting decrypted as it goes up the stack on the receiving side.

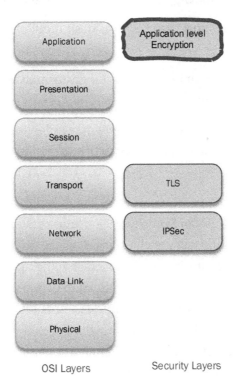

Figure 6-3. *Communication Security*

Virtual Private Network

Virtual Private Networks (VPNs) provide a mechanism to extend corporate, school, and home networks to remote, untrusted networks such that a device connected from a remote network is functionally connected to the private network. The device encrypts all the network data, and the data travels through the untrusted Internet in an encrypted fashion. Once the data reaches the edge of the private network, the data is decrypted at the edge and sent to the nodes in the private network. More specifically, it allows enterprise users, corporate users, and users of big organizations to connect to their parent networks through untrusted networks, like the Internet. There are three big categories of VPNs that are commonly used:

1. Connecting host to network as described in the preceding

2. Connecting two networks together through an untrusted network

3. Connecting two disparate networks following different network protocols or IP addressing schemes

Over the years, many protocols have been used to accomplish VPN, but today Internet Protocol Security (IPSec) and versions of TLS are used for setting up these secure channels. The use of TLS for VPN is managed by the operating system in contrast to the application managing a TLS session. In other words, with application ownership of TLS, every application will have one or more unique TLS sessions with one or more servers, and it is the application's responsibility to set up and tear down the session and make sure that the data being sent is sent through the TLS session. In contrast, a TLS VPN covers the whole client. All applications on the node can send data naturally without worrying about the TLS, and the

OS ensures that the data is always sent through the TLS connection. These (application and VPN) are two separate ways of using TLS, which are not necessarily interchangeable for given usage.

IP Security

IPSec, Internet Protocol Security, is a protocol that works at the IP layer and secures the data in the network channels. One of the foundations of the VPN is it works at the network layer to provide a secure communication channel from the source node to a network. Like TLS, the fundamental mechanisms in IPSec are the same, a key establishment/exchange protocol followed by data transmission that is encrypted and integrity protected with symmetric keys. Unlike TLS, IPSec works at the network layer, while TLS works at the transport layer. The difference is what part of the data header and data payload is encrypted and integrity protected. Like TLS, IPSec also has various modes for authenticating endpoints and protecting data.

Writing Secure Programs: Where Do We Start?

A lot has been written about secure programing and secure software. In this section, we talk about the fundamentals and provide some pointers to find more information. First, no program or code runs in isolation. It always depends on its environment, a set of libraries, a set of APIs, and sometimes software running on a remote server that this program interacts with. Hence, the security of the environment has a direct bearing on the security of the program itself. Even in these scenarios, there are certain fundamental security tenets that most programmers can use:

1. Every program has inputs and outputs; it is important to make sure that all the inputs are checked for an allowed range and any input out of range is rejected.

2. Establish boundaries of trust. This will ensure that a vulnerability in one part of the program will not be used to compromise other parts of the program.

3. Programs that use cryptography should never implement their own cryptographic functions. It is strongly recommended to use existing cryptographic libraries for cryptographic primitives. It has been repeatedly shown that cryptographic functions are extremely hard to get right, so it is recommended to stick to proven libraries that have survived the test of time.

4. Memory allocated in the heap or the stack should be carefully managed and range checked and eventually freed. Memory overflows are one of the topmost causes of vulnerabilities. Programming languages that provide automatic memory management and garbage collection, so-called manage environments (e.g., C#, Java, Python), are more resilient to these kinds of attacks than languages that expect the programmer to explicitly manage memory (e.g., C, C++).

5. It is the responsibility of the programmer to ensure that any logs generated do not have any secrets, since logs are generally not access controlled.

6. Compiler warnings are our friends. Sometimes compiler warnings point us to hidden vulnerabilities; always try to fix the compiler warnings before shipping the code.

7. Adhere to the principle of least privilege. If a function or subroutine does not need access to a certain variable, restrict it from the function to prevent any unintended modifications of the variable.

8. When there are multiple people working on the same program, have a secure coding standard so things remain simple and do not get cloaked in multiple styles or standards of coding.

9. Run static and dynamic analysis tools to remove any inadvertent errors that are not caught by compilers.

10. It always helps to have a second pair of eyes review the code.

11. Lastly, always have a recovery plan ready. Attackers will find vulnerabilities, and they will compromise your program. There must be a way to fix the vulnerability and update the new program in the field.

Summary

Computer security has become an integral part of computer science. It not only impacts our data; in some cases, it can impact our physical safety. As the threats in the ecosystem are evolving, the industry is developing new countermeasures to diffuse these threats. However, there is no silver bullet that can counter all threats, and we need a mixed set of tools in our arsenal to protect us from these emerging threats. The fundamental cornerstones of computer security, access control and cryptography, are likely to evolve in coming years. As outlined previously, passwords are on their way out, albeit slowly, and are increasingly likely to get replaced with biometrics-based techniques. We can expect use of more encrypted network channels, VPNs (Virtual Private Networks), or TLS (Transport Layer Security) as the network data increases. The need for DRM (Digital Rights Management) is going to increase as the media industry pours billions into new and exciting content. Privacy will be the key debate for the next decade due to multiple economic factors like advertisement revenue that enables service providers to provide *free services* to users in exchange for user information. Finally, state actors are likely to use cyber warfare to complement traditional warfare, and there will be an increased need for encryption mechanisms that can be *managed by* law enforcement authorities. One thing is clear: computer security as we know it today will transform in a positive manner in the coming years.

References and Further Reading

- A. Acquisti, C. Taylor, and L. Wagman. "The economics of privacy." *Journal of Economic Literature*. 2016, doi: 10.1257/jel.54.2.442

- C. Dwork and A. Roth. "The algorithmic foundations of differential privacy." *Found. Trends Theor. Comput. Sci.*, 2013, doi: 10.1561/0400000042

- C. Paar and J. Pelzl. *Understanding Cryptography*. 2010

- J. Daemen and V. Rijmen. "The Design of Rijndael." *New York*, 2002

- M. E. Smid and D. K. Branstad. "The Data Encryption Standard: Past and Future." *Proc. IEEE*, 1988, doi: 10.1109/5.4441

- NIST. "SHA-3 Standard: Permutation-Based Hash and Extendable-Output Functions." 2015

- N. H. Function *et al.* "Description of SHA-256, SHA-384 and SHA-512." *ACM Trans. Program. Lang. Syst.*, 2016

- R. L. Rivest, A. Shamir, and L. Adleman. "A Method for Obtaining Digital Signatures and Public-Key Cryptosystems." *Commun. ACM*, vol. 21, no. 2, 1978, doi: 10.1145/359340.359342

- W. Diffie, W. Diffie, and M. E. Hellman. "New Directions in Cryptography." *IEEE Trans. Inf. Theory*, vol. 22, no. 6, 1976, doi: 10.1109/TIT.1976.1055638

- D. Johnson, A. Menezes, and S. Vanstone, "The Elliptic Curve Digital Signature Algorithm (ECDSA)." *Int. J. Inf. Secur.*, 2001, doi: 10.1007/s102070100002

- G. M. Lentner and P. Parycek. "Electronic identity (eID) and electronic signature (eSig) for eGovernment services – a comparative legal study." *Transform. Gov. People, Process Policy*, 2016, doi: 10.1108/TG-11-2013-0047

- D. Cooper, S. Santesson, S. Farrell, S. Boeyen, R. Housley, and W. Polk. "Internet X.509 Public Key Infrastructure Certificate and Certificate Revocation List (CRL) Profile." 2008

- E. Skoudis and L. Zeltser. *Malware: Fighting Malicious Code*. Pearson, 2003

- C. Fachkha and M. Debbabi. "Darknet as a Source of Cyber Intelligence: Survey, Taxonomy, and Characterization." *IEEE Commun. Surv. Tutorials*, 2016, doi: 10.1109/COMST.2015.2497690

- H. Orman. "The Morris Worm." *Secur. Privacy, IEEE*, 2011

- P. Kocher *et al.* "Spectre attacks: Exploiting speculative execution." 2019, doi: 10.1109/SP.2019.00002

- J. Corbet, A. Rubini, and G. Kroah-Hartman. "Linux Device Drivers, Third Edition." *Linux Device Drivers, Third Edition*, 2005

- A. Kadav and M. M. Swift. "Understanding modern device drivers." 2012, doi: 10.1145/2150976.2150987

- S. Ghorbani Lyastani, M. Schilling, M. Neumayr, M. Backes, and S. Bugiel. "Is FIDO2 the kingslayer of user authentication? a comparative usability study of FIDO2 passwordless authentication." 2020, doi: 10.1109/SP40000.2020.00047

- J. Gerhardt-Powals and M. H. Powals. "The digital millennium copyright act." *ACM SIGCSE Bull.*, 1999, doi: 10.1145/384267.305937

- S. Rose, O. Borchert, S. Mitchell, and S. Connelly. "Zero Trust Architecture." *Nist*, 2019.

CHAPTER 7

Cloud Computing

We discussed in the earlier chapters that in a distributed system, there are two parts: client and server. Traditionally, corporations have managed their back-end servers on their own at their physical premise. However, there is a trend to consolidate these resources and services elsewhere (the cloud) on a network. These services can be used by the client systems as needed, and the resources can be remotely shared and optimized. The services are provided and managed by "cloud service providers" (CSPs). In this chapter, we'll discuss different cloud computing models, their implications, and trade-offs. We'll follow that up with different deployment configurations and consideration for developing and deploying portable and interoperable cloud solutions.

Note Simply speaking, cloud computing is a mechanism that delivers computing services over the Internet ("the cloud") to offer faster innovation and dynamic scaling. It can help lower the operating costs for many of the usage scenarios by means of more optimized resource utilization.

Figure 7-1 illustrates cloud computing. Essentially, the infrastructure, platform, and services are hosted in the cloud; and then customers can access these services over the Internet via various interfaces.

© Paul D. Crutcher, Neeraj Kumar Singh, and Peter Tiegs 2021
P. D. Crutcher et al., *Essential Computer Science*,
https://doi.org/10.1007/978-1-4842-7107-0_7

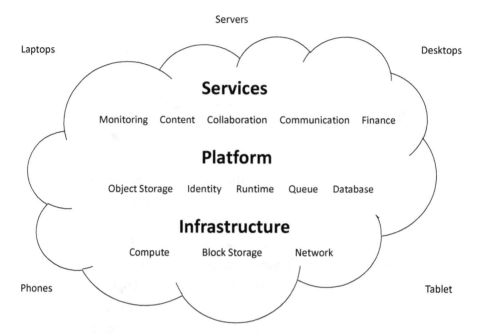

Figure 7-1. *Illustration of Cloud Computing*

Cloud Computing Models

There are different models of providing cloud computing services. Broadly speaking, these cloud computing service offerings fall into four categories: Infrastructure as a Service (IaaS), Platform as a Service (PaaS), serverless (aka Function as a Service, or FaaS for short), and Software as a Service (SaaS). Serverless (aka FaaS), however, is usually considered the same as or an extension to PaaS and not treated as a separate model in some literature. These models are also referred to as a cloud computing pyramid or stack because they build on top of one another.

Figure 7-2 depicts how the various models stack on each other. In the following sections, we'll briefly discuss these models one by one.

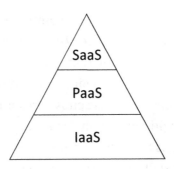

Figure 7-2. *Cloud Computing Pyramid or Stack*

IaaS

Infrastructure as a Service (IaaS) is the most basic and flexible model of cloud computing. Essentially, IaaS provides a virtualized computing infrastructure that is provisioned, managed, and accessed over the Internet. Virtualization is a mechanism of creating virtual computer hardware like CPU, storage, network, and so on. An IaaS provider manages the physical end of the infrastructure (compute, storage, memory, and network) in a shared data center and lets their customers customize and use those virtualized resources to suit their needs.

The other way to look at IaaS is that the cloud service customer (CSC) rents the hardware resources from a cloud service provider (CSP). The hardware is hosted and managed by the CSP. It is essentially like a customer getting a machine with the requested hardware – compute, storage, memory, and network – from the CSP accessible over the network. The customer is responsible for the rest of the infrastructure management (OS, software, security, etc.).

IaaS provides dynamic scaling up and down based on the demand that lets customers pay only for what they use. Because compute resources are subscribed, purchased, and used as a service, it helps customers avoid the upfront cost and complexity of procuring and managing their own physical servers and other related infrastructure. Each part of computing resources is offered as a separate service component, and then the customer can choose and assemble required compute resources. For instance, customers can choose the number of CPUs, memory, storage, and networks separately based on their need, and the CSP will assemble and make a virtual system with those chosen resources. The resources need to be subscribed and rented only for as long as needed. The cloud service provider manages the virtual hardware infrastructure, while customers purchase, install, configure, and manage their own software pieces like operating systems, middleware, and applications. Microsoft Azure, Amazon Web Services (AWS), and Google Compute Engine (GCE) are examples of IaaS.

IaaS services make it super quick and easy to get access to hardware resources; you don't have to procure, provision, and secure the hardware. Given the control and flexibility of software deployment in this environment, IaaS is the most efficient (in terms of time, cost, and flexibility) for exploration work. Also, owing to the flexibility, IaaS is always available for scenarios where the other services like PaaS and SaaS are unavailable.

It is also to be noted that when customers use more value-added cloud services from a CSP, they are charged extra for those value additions. For instance, PaaS is more value-added service than IaaS because CSPs are responsible for more services as part of PaaS than IaaS. So a corollary of that is IaaS will be cheaper than PaaS for same level of usage.

PaaS

Platform as a Service sits a little bit higher up the pyramid than IaaS. That means, as part of PaaS offering, the CSPs are responsible for, and maintain, more services than in an IaaS model. As part of PaaS, CSPs supply an on-demand environment for developing, testing, delivering, and managing software services. PaaS makes it easier for developers to quickly create solutions without worrying about setting up or managing the underlying infrastructure of hardware and software needed for development and deployment. AWS Elastic Beanstalk, Apache Stratos, and Google App Engine are some examples of PaaS.

PaaS offers everything that IaaS provides – that is, the underlying infrastructure as the service. However, in addition to the hardware, PaaS consists of middleware, framework, and other development and deployment tools. As part of PaaS, the cloud service providers provide these platform ingredients (tools and software). So the customers can focus on their development rather than trying to manage the SW and HW infrastructure.

Serverless

Serverless computing is an extension to PaaS. This is also known as "Function as a Service" (FaaS). FaaS allows customers to execute code when needed without having to allocate computing resources in advance. In other models like IaaS and PaaS, the user has to allocate the computing resources in advance. As with PaaS, the cloud provider manages the complete infrastructure. This allows the customer to focus on deploying application code in the form of "functions." FaaS enables your functions to scale up or down automatically to meet demand, which makes FaaS an excellent fit for workloads that fluctuate in terms of resource requirement.

Essentially, serverless architectures are highly scalable and event driven, only using resources needed to fill the given demand. Customers only pay for the resources they consume; therefore, serverless (FaaS) is the truest form of "pay-as-you-use" cloud computing model. Some examples of serverless are AWS Lambda and Azure Functions.

The serverless usage model is best suited for burst, trigger-based usage scenarios and can support extremely high throughput. The customer does not have to care or preplan for the infrastructure. The CSP infrastructure will automagically provision the platform and deploy and run the code when there is a trigger. There are many organizations, for example,

Thomson Reuters, the Coca-Cola Company, Netflix, and so on, that are already leveraging serverless effectively.

SaaS

Software as a service (SaaS) is the model where software applications are delivered for use as needed over the Internet. Applications are typically made available on a subscription basis. With SaaS, cloud providers host and manage the software application including the required infrastructure and maintenance, including software upgrades and security patching. Customers just use the software application, over the Internet, without worrying about any aspect of development, deployment, and maintenance of the software.

SaaS sits at the top of the pyramid, and for the majority, it is the most familiar form of cloud computing. Some examples of SaaS include Microsoft Office 365, Salesforce, and Gmail.

SaaS is where the customers are not bothered by or responsible for any other aspects of software except that it should be reliably available when needed in a secure fashion. The service provider is responsible for everything. This is the only practical model for individual end users. However, there are organizations that don't want to develop, deploy, and maintain their own software application for a specific purpose and so buy a subscription and let their employees use it. This allows organizations to focus on their core business rather than be distracted by other needs.

Comparison of Cloud Computing Models

Figure 7-3 shows you the split responsibilities between the cloud service provider and the cloud service customer across IaaS, PaaS, and SaaS. As it is evident, the management responsibility of the CSC goes up from IaaS to PaaS to SaaS. Roughly speaking, in the IaaS model, the user gets the hardware equivalent of compute resource and everything else is managed by the user, while in the SaaS case, pretty much everything is managed by the service provider and the user just needs to use the software.

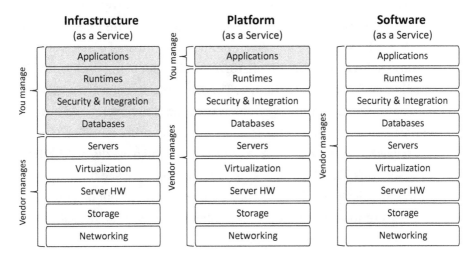

Figure 7-3. *Service Management Responsibility Chart Across IaaS, PaaS, and SaaS*

Benefits of Cloud Computing

As we've discussed, there is a lot of traction and movement to cloud computing. Organizations either have adopted or are in the process of defining the cloud strategy for optimal benefits. Much of traction is for good reason. Cloud computing offers organizations many benefits, which we will discuss next.

Cost

In the cloud computing world, the customers use computing resources provided by the cloud service provider. Cloud computing eliminates the capital expense of buying hardware and software, physical hosting of hardware, and setting up and running on-site data centers. The capital cost is completely taken away and born by the cloud service providers. The same is true for operating and management costs of the computing resources and other accessories like the electricity for power and cooling.

The customer must be aware that nothing comes for free. CSPs charge customers for the services they offer. Practically, in most of cases, the amortized cost for the customer will turn out cheaper using the cloud than hosting their own infrastructure. There are some scenarios where it could be costlier to use cloud services as compared to hosting one's own data center. However, even in those cases, there are other benefits of using cloud services vs. hosting one's own data center, which we discuss in the following sections. Finally, as this ecosystem evolves, we see that it is more and more likely that large corporations will have a split of cloud and on-premises compute infrastructure that can be combined, in a so-called hybrid cloud, to get the best of both worlds.

Scalability

Another key benefit of cloud computing service is the ability to scale dynamically. There are multiple use cases where the computing needs may be bursty in nature. For instance, during festival time, there could be a lot more load on the ecommerce websites than otherwise. Similarly, for a geography-specific service, there could be more load in daytime than at midnight. So dynamic scalability refers to the ability of cloud to deploy the right amount of resources like computing power, storage, and bandwidth as per demand.

The other very important side effect of dynamic scalability is that the customer need not plan for and buy worst-case workload. It just scales as needed. The CSPs do charge for enabling dynamic scaling; however, given the benefits, it is totally worth it.

Velocity

As the cloud computing resources are already pooled at the CSPs and services are provided on demand, practically all computing resources can be provisioned quickly, in minutes in fact. This facility is in complete contrast to the procuring hardware resource and deploying in the traditional data center world, which can take months, if not quarters, to complete. This capability enables great flexibility for customers and takes off the pressure of capacity planning.

Reliability and Availability

Cloud service providers provide robust solutions for data backup, disaster recovery, and business continuity in an easier and less expensive manner. The cloud service providers add redundancy and apply modern management tools to make the cloud computing resources and overall environment reliable and available.

Productivity

Cloud computing enables high productivity for customers. For instance, with a traditional data center, setting up and managing computing resource requires a lot of time-consuming chores: hardware setup, software patching, security updates, and so on. In the cloud computing world, these chores are performed by the CSPs, so customers' IT teams can spend time on achieving more important business goals. And, because CSPs scale across thousands of customers, they develop and deploy automated modern tools for these management activities.

Another aspect of improved productivity for customers is a result of velocity; since the required computing resources can be provisioned and deployed almost instantly, the customer can begin prototyping immediately.

In addition to velocity, cloud computing has various differing levels of services: from IaaS to SaaS. The customer may choose what they want to focus on and leverage rest as a service from the CSP. All in all, cloud computing brings productivity across the board.

Performance

The most prominent cloud service providers are deployed worldwide. They apply secure and fast networks and apply the latest technologies to secure their data and upgrade the hardware resources (compute, storage, memory, etc.) regularly with the latest generation of fast and efficient computing hardware. These attributes make best-in-class performance available to cloud service customers all around the world, reducing latency for geo-dispersed customers by means of colocating the cloud resources and customer in the same geography.

Ease of Use and Maintenance

Cloud service providers offer several tools, technologies, and controls to strengthen the security and protection of data and apps. Additionally, the cloud service providers keep the security patches, features, and tools up to date, which results in improved security.

Combined with other benefits, cloud computing makes software development, deployment, and maintenance easy, hassle-free, and secure while being economical.

Cloud Deployment Configurations

So far, we've talked about what cloud computing is in general and the benefits it brings. When it comes to deploying to the cloud, there are many ways to implement that. There are many different decisions that could impact the implementation and the deployment, which makes one instance of cloud deployment look very different from another. Some such decisions include whom the cloud is accessible to, where it is located and hosted, how the security is implemented, and so on.

Broadly, there are three different ways to deploy cloud services: private cloud, public cloud, and a mix of the two called hybrid cloud. In the following sections, we will talk about each of them and their related trade-offs.

Private Cloud

A private cloud refers to a setup where the cloud computing resources are designed and used exclusively by a single organization. The private cloud usually resides behind a firewall and on a private network. A completely on-premises private cloud can be physically located on the on-site data center. The organization may host and manage the private cloud on their own. However, some organizations hire third-party service providers to host their private cloud.

Private cloud solutions offer both security and control. The benefits, however, come at a cost. The organizations that own the cloud are responsible for the creation, deployment, and management of all the infrastructure and software, which makes the private cloud a less economical model than the public cloud in most of the cases. The private cloud could still make sense for the businesses with very stringent regulatory requirements.

Public Cloud

As the name suggests, public clouds are owned and operated by third-party service providers, known as cloud service providers (CSPs). These cloud service providers deliver computing resources over the Internet for their subscribers. Amazon, Microsoft, and Google are some examples of public cloud service providers. These cloud service providers specialize in the business and own and manage all hardware, software, and other supporting infrastructure. The customers of cloud service providers subscribe to and access these services over the Internet. Because of the sharing of cloud resources across the customers, public cloud offerings may be more economical for the majority of customers and use cases. The public cloud model provides smaller organizations the benefits of scale and economy.

Hybrid Cloud

A hybrid cloud, as one can guess, combines public and private clouds. The hybrid cloud is designed to allow two platforms to work together, seamlessly. The hybrid cloud model brings the best of both worlds (private cloud and public cloud) together: provide the scalable computing power of a public cloud with the security and control of a private cloud.

Ideal Cloud Deployment Configuration

As we discussed in the preceding sections, there is a trade-off between the public and private cloud deployment configurations. For example, the private cloud configuration may give you control and may be better equipped to store sensitive information regarding the corporation. The public deployment may provide better flexibility and scale. The performance and uptime may be better for public cloud deployment because the public cloud service providers specialize in that.

The use case itself may define whether a public or private cloud deployment is more suitable. For instance, there may be scope for optimization in terms of data going into (ingress)/and going out of (egress) the private cloud setups on-premises, while with public setups, there could be potentially increased cost for such data movement.

Because of these reasons, many larger organizations combine the benefits of the two and use a hybrid cloud deployment. There is no standard guidance on what mix (private vs. public cloud) is the ideal. Organizations need to carefully evaluate and come up with the ideal setup based on their usages and trade-offs. In some cases, it could even require a multi-cloud model.

Multi-cloud Model

In cases where a single public cloud isn't enough to meet an organization's computing needs, they may have to use services from multiple public cloud service providers and deploy a little more complex hybrid cloud architecture that combines a private cloud with multiple public cloud services. This model of deployment is known as multi-cloud. While a hybrid cloud consists of a public and a private cloud, a multi-cloud environment is a lot more complex and engages multiple public cloud service providers.

Cloud Configuration Interface/Mechanism

In the earlier sections, we talked in detail about cloud services, the complex deployment models, benefits, and so on. Although all of that might seem very fancy, at the most basic level, accessing cloud services is not very different from accessing a remote system over a network. On top of that, the CSPs may provide more user-friendly ways to access and manage the services.

However, before we can access anything, we need to subscribe to the cloud services offered by the CSP. Once you have the subscription, the CSP will provide a user interface to create a logical custom machine by assembling computing resources like CPU, memory, storage, and so on. Once the machine is ready and the network address is allocated, it's pretty much like accessing any remote system over a network.

Note   To lure customers, CSPs may provide free access for some limited usage and time period.

At a high level, cloud computing is made of two components: front end and back end. The front end enables the customers to subscribe to, manage, and access the cloud services provided by the cloud service provider. The back end is the actual cloud, and it is made of the resources (compute, memory, storage, network, etc.) that are required to enable and support cloud computing services.

Figure 7-4 provides a logical view for interfacing with cloud services and resources.

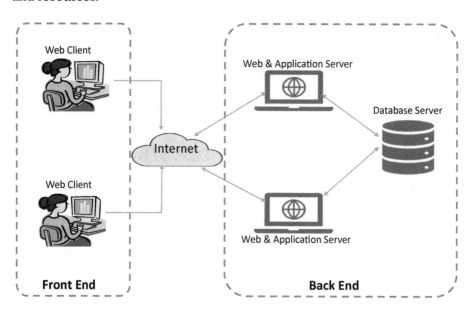

Figure 7-4. *Logical View of Interfacing with Cloud*

Note   Logically, using cloud services is similar to accessing a remote machine over a network.

Cloud Service Providers

The following are several cloud service providers (CSPs) in the market today. This list is not meant to be comprehensive and by no means in any specific priority order:

- Google Cloud

- Microsoft Azure

- Amazon AWS

- Alibaba Cloud

- IBM

- Oracle

- And many more, like Linode, VMware, and so on

Considerations in Choosing a CSP

As we saw in the preceding section, there are a variety of cloud service providers. Although most of them provide similar capabilities and services, most CSPs offer proprietary and nonstandard (e.g., open source) services, supported by proprietary architectures and technologies. Choosing to use these proprietary services and technologies and developing solutions using them might lead to customers getting locked in with the CSP. The lock-in could happen due to various reasons including

- Using custom CSP solutions, services, and mechanisms

- Defining architectural decisions based on specific services by the CSP

- Designing and developing with the specific CSP in consideration

The resulting lock-in could lead to several negative side effects, for instance:

- Significant cost, time, and effort during migration

- Potential downtime during migration

- Difficulty migrating to a different, lower-cost CSP in the future

With various cloud computing models, lock-in risk levels are different across IaaS, SaaS, and PaaS. For example, let's talk about PaaS. A specific PaaS platform from a CSP may support only limited and proprietary technologies, for example, specific web frameworks, languages, databases, and so on. This can lead to development of application architecture that is tied to the technologies offered by that specific CSP resulting in the application getting locked in the CSP. Again, across IaaS, PaaS, and SaaS, the lock-in risk is lowest in the IaaS model because IaaS functionality is broadly similar and there are several standards covering them.

However, one may ask why lock-in is a bad thing. Why would one need to migrate from one CSP to another? The argument could be that while choosing a CSP for the very first time, we perform due diligence to choose the best CSP for the specific need and use case. Once we do that, what is the need of ever considering migrating? In the following section, we will discuss what causes customers to move from one CSP to other.

Motivation for Switching CSPs

It is evident that cloud service customers (CSCs) evaluate CSPs at the time of choosing and make the best choice based on their particular use case and data available. However, requirements can change quickly, and that can be motivation for moving from one CSP to another. Some of the reasons that could cause the need for migration are covered in the following sections. These reasons are not meant to be comprehensive, but simply some of the most common ones.

Usage and Pricing Change

One of the primary reasons for a customer moving from one CSP to other relates to a usage and/or pricing change.

The CSPs have a pricing model, and when a customer evaluates the CSPs for pricing, they use a model for usage levels and patterns. However, actual usage could turn out to be very different than the original model, and that could make the original evaluation very far from reality. It may turn out that for the actual usage model, a different CSP may be more economical.

Also, usage could evolve and change because of the services deployed on the cloud becoming more or less popular than originally anticipated.

The other potential reason is that the CSPs revise their fees from time to time, and based on these revisions, the current CSP might become less attractive than some other.

CSP Ecosystem Change

The other category of changes that could lead to a customer moving from one CSP to another relates to changes in the CSP ecosystem itself. Some of those include

- CSPs Moving In and Out of Business: Although rare for some of the big players in the CSP business, some of the smaller ones may move out of business or change hands. Also, like the CSPs moving out of business, there could be a scenario where a new CSP emerges and may have better offerings in terms of pricing, scalability, and support.

- CSP Abandoning a Specific Service: The overall cloud computing services and offerings are evolving as we speak, and as a side effect of that, the CSPs may abandon or change specific proprietary offerings.

Regulatory, Privacy, and Business Dynamics Change

Another category that could motivate changing CSPs is related to regulatory, privacy, and business dynamics changes:

- Rules, Regulations, and Policy: There could be a government regulation or other policy changes that could dictate hosting of certain services in certain geographies or a specific way that in turn results in need for moving from one CSP to another.

- Discovery of a New Vulnerability/Loophole or Limitation at a CSP: While in deployment, the customer could realize/discover a new vulnerability, loophole, or limitation that would require the customer to move to another CSP.

- Business Dynamics Change: The business environment is fluid, and things change quickly. So, for instance, the CSP and CSC could move into the same business, and then there could be some conflict of interest in hosting/supporting the data from competition.

Considerations for Developing Portable and Interoperable Cloud Solutions

As we've discussed in earlier sections, it's evident that cloud service customers (CSCs) may need to move from one CSP to another. That directly implies that one must develop solutions in a way that they are portable and interoperable across CSPs. In the following sections, we will talk about what we mean by portability and interoperability, as well as mechanisms we can apply to achieve this.

Interoperability vs. Portability

Generally speaking, interoperability can be thought as the measurement of the degree to which diverse systems or components can work together successfully.

In cloud computing context, there are two parties: cloud service customer and cloud service provider. They both interact over a network connection using a prescribed interface or API. There are different aspects of the cloud service, and there are typically separate interfaces for dealing with these different aspects of the cloud service.

For instance, there could be functional interfaces of the cloud service itself, interfaces for authentication and authorization, interfaces for administration of the cloud services, and even more interfaces relating to such business aspects as billing and invoicing. The objective of interoperability is that these interfaces are standardized in a way that they are interoperable so that there is minimal impact to the CSC's component while moving from one CSP to other.

Similarly, portability refers to the ability of a customer to move and adapt their applications (application portability) and data (data portability)

- Between a customer system and CSP

- From one CSP to another CSP

Portability is important because the lack of it leads to considerable cost and effort when you do have to change systems. There are two aspects of portability that need consideration:

- **Cloud data portability** is the ability to easily transfer data: from one CSP to another and between a CSP and customer's system.

- **Cloud application portability** is the ability to easily transfer an application or application component: from one CSP to another and between a CSP and customer's system. This typically only applies to IaaS and PaaS services, since in the case of a SaaS service, the application belongs to the cloud service provider and there is no use case of that being ported elsewhere by the customer.

As per the *Cloud Standards Customer Council's Interoperability and Portability for Cloud Computing: A Guide Version 2.0* (2017), the interoperability and portability aspects of the cloud solution could pictorially be depicted as in Figure 7-5.

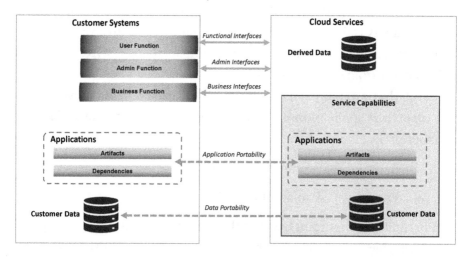

Figure 7-5. *Elements of Interoperability and Portability in Cloud Services*

In Figure 7-5, the first three interfaces relate to the interoperability aspect, while the rest relate to the portability aspect of the cloud services.

Interoperability Challenges

There are several reasons why interoperability challenges exist across CSPs. The key reason is interfaces and services offered by CSPs are not standardized. Different cloud service providers use different APIs even for comparable cloud services. The greatest level of interoperability is made available by IaaS, while the PaaS cloud services have lower levels of interoperability because there are few interface standards for PaaS. Recently, open source platforms such as Cloud Foundry are gaining momentum and provide common open source–based solutions that can run on any CSP platform. Similarly, SaaS applications present the greatest interoperability challenge. That is because there are very few standards for SaaS applications. Therefore, moving from one SaaS application to another SaaS application usually requires interface changes.

To mitigate these challenges, the cloud service customer usually has an isolation or mapping layer between their own applications and the cloud service interface. For instance, technologies such as enterprise service buses (ESBs) can be used to build these isolation layers. The other potential mitigation option is to use the services offered by an inter-cloud provider (aka cloud service broker), who maps a "standard" interface offered to the customer to a varying set of interfaces offered by several different CSPs.

Portability Challenges

As discussed earlier, the portability challenges are different across IaaS, PaaS, and SaaS. The biggest challenges are for applications built for PaaS platforms, because

- Platforms can vary widely between different CSPs.

- The app environment can differ substantially across CSPs.

For example, to be scalable and elastic, a PaaS platform may enforce a specific way to manage data that may not be supported by other PaaS platforms. Although there are some standards relating to PaaS that are picking up momentum, for IaaS cloud services, there are several standards that are already in practice. Using these standards results in improved portability of applications.

To minimize the portability challenges, there are a couple of best-known strategies in place: one is increasing adoption of common open source PaaS platforms such as Cloud Foundry, and another is leveraging containerization that allows independent deployment of applications. In the following sections, we discuss containerization and orchestration and how they help enable portability.

Containers, Docker, and Kubernetes

In order to make software and applications portable, the first consideration is how we can isolate the application so that it has limited dependency on and expectation from the underlying environment it is going to be deployed on. That is where the idea of containers originated and was first implemented by Docker. Essentially, a container is a standard unit of software that packages up an application and all its dependencies so that the application runs the same, regardless of the computing environment (assuming similar compute resources are available).

Containers allow a developer to package up an application with all the parts it needs, such as libraries and other dependencies, and deploy it as one package: a container image. Container images become containers at runtime.

So, in a way, containers are like virtual machines (VMs) in terms of isolation benefits; however, they work at a slightly different level: containers virtualize the operating system, while virtual machines virtualize the hardware. As a by-product of this difference, containers are lighter weight and efficient as compared to virtual machines.

Note   A container is a packaging of an application and its dependencies as a self-contained package, and Docker is one implementation of this concept. There is an initiative to standardize the container format for wider portability called the *Open Container Initiative*.

Figure 7-6 shows the similarity and the difference between virtual machine– and container (Docker)-based deployments.

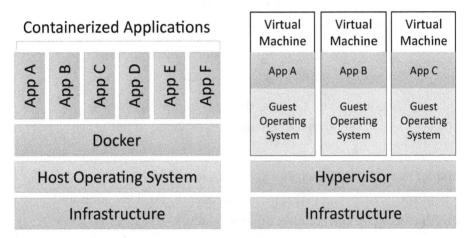

Figure 7-6. *Containers vs. Virtual Machines*

As is evident from Figure 7-6, containers are an abstraction above the OS layer that packages an application and its dependencies together. Multiple containers can run on the same machine (virtual or physical) and share the host OS kernel with each other. Each container runs as isolated processes in user space. Containers are lighter weight in terms of space and computing overhead than VMs and therefore more efficient than VMs.

Virtual machines have been around for some time now and are well known. They provide abstraction of physical hardware each running its own copy of an operating system and the applications, necessary binaries, and libraries. One or more VMs can run on the supplied hardware, but each VM has a full OS.

As such, VMs are much heavier than containers. However, they are not mutually exclusive. In fact, in today's world, both virtual machines and containers are combined to leverage the best of both. So, in practice, there could be one capable machine running multiple virtual machines, each of which in turn running more than one container as needed.

The use of containers requires three additional capabilities or tools:

- Builder: We need the tools and technology to build a container image.

- Engine: We need the tools and technology to run an image. A running image is a container.

- Orchestration: We need the tools and technology to effectively manage container instances.

The first two pieces – Builder and Engine – are very clear. We need Builder to create the image and Engine to run that image. Docker serves that purpose. Essentially, Docker is a set of command line tools and runtime to create and run the container images.

Figure 7-7 demonstrates a high-level architecture of Docker. The command line tools like "Docker build" and "Docker run" are the client. These commands are used by the end users to create and run Docker images. The Docker images created are registered to a global registry that allows an image to be built once and then used multiple times. The "Docker daemon" creates and runs the images in contained environments (containers).

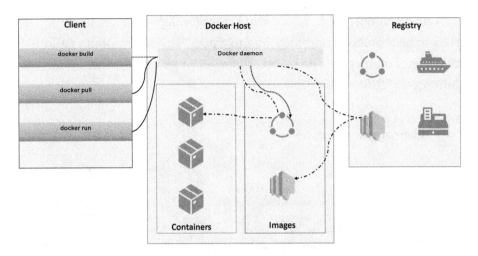

Figure 7-7. *Docker Architecture*

Containers are a portable way to bundle and run applications. However, in a production environment, we need to manage the containers that run and ensure that there is no downtime. Additionally, we need to be able to scale the number of containers based on demand. Kubernetes (K8s) does exactly that. It standardizes the process of deploying and managing the sets of containers that are required for a given application.

Note   Kubernetes is a container orchestration framework that manages deployment of containers to provide resiliency to the system.

Figure 7-8 shows the high-level Kubernetes architecture. At the top layer, there is the command line interface (CLI), "kubectl," that works with the control plane to orchestrate the deployment. Kubernetes nodes manage and run pods. The nodes could either be virtual or physical machines. A node can host and manage one or more pods. Each of these pods can run one or more containers. From the Kubernetes perspective, pods are the unit of deployment. There could be pods with

219

just one container; however, for more complex deployments, there is likely to be more than one container to a pod. "kubelet" monitors and manages containers within a pod. All these pieces put together is called a Kubernetes "cluster."

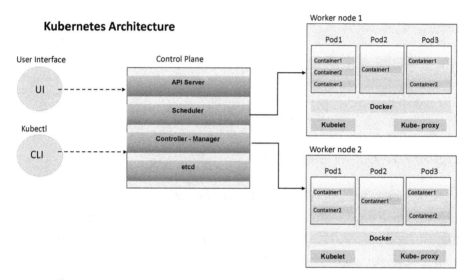

Figure 7-8. *Kubernetes architecture*

Benefits of Containers and Container Orchestration

Although we talked about containers, Docker, and Kubernetes in the context of portability, which clearly is one of the most important benefits of using containers, there are other benefits. The key ones are described next.

Security

First and foremost, it adds extra security through isolation. While the isolation and the security can be architected by the virtual machines as well, however, since containers include only the necessary code and libraries needed by the application, they have less code to be compromised, compared to VMs.

Scalability

Applying microservices, containers, and container orchestration together, we can automatically scale up and down the application resources based on the demand. For illustration, during the festive season when the demand and load on the ecommerce portal, say Amazon, grows, more instances of microservice-based containers can be automatically created by Kubernetes to bear the load.

The Way Forward

The cloud movement is still relatively young by technology standards and is still rapidly evolving. How this evolution will impact the ecosystem is anyone's guess. That said, with faster and faster networks and throughput, we are headed to a world where everything goes into/through the cloud. All the applications and services reside in the cloud (public, private, and/ or hybrid). For example, one has moved to the cloud-based "Office 365." This model enables use of SaaS and pay-per-use.

There are several other factors in play while defining the future of clients and clouds. First and foremost, even though there is wider availability of the Internet across the globe, there still is a large portion of the population that is not yet well connected with the Internet. Even for the population where there is reasonable Internet access, bandwidth and throughput are not always great enough to make it a seamless experience.

Additionally, there are new uses that require real-time responses. For a real-time response, going back and forth between the cloud and client over a network may not be performant, so clients still need reasonable compute power. For instance, in gaming and other interactive applications, the experience would be compromised if we fully relied on the cloud for all the processing.

Finally, data protection and privacy concerns could prevent users from doing everything in the cloud.

So, in summary, the smart clients are not going away anytime soon. In fact, they are going to co-exist and continue their symbiotic relationship with the cloud.

Leading organizations have already realized they need both robust client and cloud solutions working together and have started creating architectures to provide the best experience for users. Specifically, the idea is to look at the ways we can leverage the capabilities of both client and cloud in developing a solution and offload the services at the client or cloud, respectively, whichever is more efficient for the job.

Recommendations

Based on the discussion on portability and interoperability, we would like to consolidate the key recommendations for cloud service customers, as follows:

- Portability and interoperability should be key considerations when choosing the CSP. Also, the portability and interoperability requirements should be part of the agreement with the CSP.

- Use open and standard technologies, protocols, and mechanisms, and avoid using CSP proprietary solutions, where practical. Choose a CSP that supports these open and standard technologies.

- Ensure applications follow service-orientated architecture (SOA) and employ standard APIs for interoperability. Additionally, use protocol adapters like enterprise service buses for handling protocol mismatches.

- Leverage containers for virtualizing applications and artifacts to ensure portability.

Summary

In this chapter, we presented the fundamentals of cloud computing, its benefits, and the various potential deployment configurations and why choose one over another. We introduced a few of the cloud service providers (CSPs) in business today, as well as the key considerations in choosing a cloud service provider for a specific use case or organization. We emphasized the need for portability and interoperability as first-order criteria to avoid lock-in to a specific CSP. We also covered how to develop portable and interoperable solutions before closing with a brief conversation on how the client and cloud will potentially evolve in the future.

References and Further Reading

- *European Journal of ePractice.* Three Dimensions of Organizational Interoperability: `www.epractice.eu/files/6.1.pdf`

- Cloud Standards Customer Council (2017). Practical Guide to Cloud Computing: `www.cloud-council.org/deliverables/practical-guide-to-cloud-computing.htm`

- Cloud Standards Customer Council (2015). Practical Guide to Cloud Service Level Agreements: `www.cloud-council.org/deliverables/practical-guide-to-cloud-service-agreements.htm`

- Cloud Standards Customer Council (2016). Public Cloud Service Agreements: What to Expect and What to Negotiate: `www.cloud-council.org/deliverables/public-cloud-service-agreements-what-to-expect-and-whatto-negotiate.htm`

- Cloud Standards Customer Council (2016). Practical Guide to Hybrid Cloud Computing: www.cloud-council.org/deliverables/practical-guide-to-hybrid-cloud-computing.htm

- ISO/IEC 19941 Cloud Computing – Interoperability and Portability: www.iso.org/standard/66639.html

- Cloud Standards Customer Council (2017). Practical Guide to Cloud Management Platforms: www.cloud-council.org/deliverables/practical-guide-to-cloud-management-platforms.htm

- Cloud Standards Customer Council (2013). Migrating Applications to Public Cloud Services: Roadmap for Success: www.cloud-council.org/deliverables/migrating-applications-to-public-cloud-services-roadmapfor-success.htm

- Production-Grade Container Orchestration: https://kubernetes.io/

- Containers and Dockers: www.docker.com/resources/what-container

- *Open Container Initiative:* www.opencontainers.org/

- *Open Virtualization Format:* www.dmtf.org/standards/ovf

- Cloud Foundry: *Cloud Application Platform:* www.cloudfoundry.org/

- *Cloud Data Management Interface (CDMI):* www.snia.org/cdmi

CHAPTER 8

Machine Learning

In earlier chapters, we discussed aspects of computer architecture and how to efficiently program and deploy software. Thus far, we've been successful getting computers to carry out what they have been programmed to accomplish. Beyond traditional programming, questions arise about whether or not computers can mimic humans in terms of intelligence and learning. In science fiction literature, there are many stories of machines taking over the world. Is this possible? Until relatively recently, these fictions have been given little credence because there are fundamental differences between how human intelligence and computing machines work. Machines act as obedient servants – working as they are explicitly programmed to accomplish a well-defined task. They did not learn and improve or develop intelligence. And that's where machine learning comes to play. Some of the most succinct descriptions of machine learning are from Stanford and McKinsey & Co. As per Stanford, "Machine learning is the science of getting computers to act without being explicitly programmed."[1] And, as per McKinsey & Co, "Machine learning is based on algorithms that can learn from data without relying on rules-based programming."[2]

---

[1]Andrew Ng, `http://mlclass.stanford.edu/#:~:text=Machine%20learning%20 is%20the%20science,understanding%20of%20the%20human%20genome.`

[2]Jacques Bughin et al., "Artificial Intelligence the Next Digital Frontier?" McKinsey Global Institute, June 2017, `www.mckinsey.com/~/media/McKinsey/ Industries/Advanced%20Electronics/Our%20Insights/How%20artificial%20 intelligence%20can%20deliver%20real%20value%20to%20companies/MGI- Artificial-Intelligence-Discussion-paper.pdf.`

© Paul D. Crutcher, Neeraj Kumar Singh, and Peter Tiegs 2021
P. D. Crutcher et al., *Essential Computer Science*,
https://doi.org/10.1007/978-1-4842-7107-0_8

Note   Fundamentally, machine learning is the science of getting computers to learn as well as, or better than, humans.

The key difference between machine learning and conventional machine intelligence is the way machines acquire intelligence. With machine learning, machines gather intelligence based on examples (data, aka experience). In the conventional machine intelligence case, machines are explicitly programmed (instructed) to behave in a certain intelligent way. So machines may still behave like intelligent agents without applying machine learning, but they do not get better with experience.

By the way, machine learning is not a completely new thing; it has evolved and started to see more usage, proliferation, and success owing to advancement in compute resource and availability of data. In the following section, we talk about evolution of machine learning.

Brief History of Machine Learning

From the very beginning of computing devices, when we thought about learning and machines, we tried to draw parallels from the understanding of how human brains work and how computing machines/algorithms work. Neurons and their associated networks (neural networks) play the foundational role in human learning process, so researchers have tried to emulate these processes in machines. This field of study is broadly known as machine learning and artificial intelligence.

The first theory on neural networks was a paper published in 1943 where neurophysiologist Warren McCulloch and mathematician Walter Pitts talked about neurons and how they work. They decided to model these neurons using an electrical circuit, creating the underlying framework for future machine learning progress.

In 1950, Alan Turing created the "Turing Test," which is a method for determining whether a computer is capable of thinking like a human being. Turing proposed that a computer can be said to possess artificial intelligence if it can mimic human responses under specific conditions. This test is simple: for a computer to qualify as having artificial intelligence, it must be able to convince a human that it is a human and not a computer. The test was originally named "The Imitation Game."

Arthur Samuel in 1952 created the first computer program that could learn as it ran. It was a game that played checkers. Later in 1958, Frank Rosenblatt designed the first artificial neural network to recognize patterns and shapes. Then in 1959, Bernard Widrow and Marcian Hoff created two neural network models at Stanford University. The first was called ADALINE, and it could detect binary patterns. The other one (which was the next generation) was called MADALINE. MADALINE was used to eliminate echo on phone lines – so the first useful real-world application of machine learning, MADALINE, came into use and continues to be used today.

Despite the success of MADALINE, there was not much progress until the late 1970s for many reasons. Recently, both the amount of data available and exponential growth in processing capabilities, neural networks, and other ML technologies have become viable.

Artificial Intelligence, Machine Learning, and Deep Learning

We use the terms artificial intelligence, machine learning, and deep learning a lot. Is there a difference between them? At times, we seem to use these terms interchangeably, but it is important to understand that they are related and not interchangeable. We define each one in the following.

Artificial intelligence (AI) refers to intelligence demonstrated by machines. In other words, artificial intelligence refers to the simulation of intelligent behavior in computers or the capability of a machine to imitate intelligent human behavior. It is used broadly to refer to any algorithms, methods, or technologies that make a system act and behave like a human. It employs machine learning, computer vision, natural language processing, cognitive robotics, and other related technologies.

Machine learning is a subfield of artificial intelligence that uses algorithms that improve with experience or learn the rules without explicitly being programmed.

Deep learning is a technique of machine learning that uses multilevel (deep) neural networks for learning. Figure 8-1 represents the relationship between the three. It illustrates that deep learning is a subfield of machine learning that is a subfield of artificial intelligence.

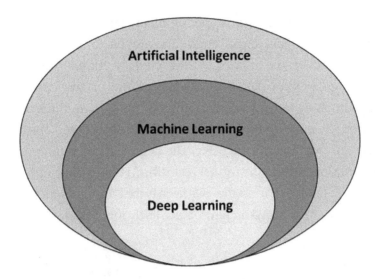

Figure 8-1. *Relationship Between Artificial Intelligence, Machine Learning, and Deep Learning*

Fundamental Tenets of Machine Learning

Having discussed machine learning and its evolution earlier, we now discuss the key tenets of machine learning. In machine learning, machines learn with data to detect patterns and rules to

- Categorize like objects.

- Predict likely outcomes based on identified (learned) rules.

- Identify patterns and relationships.

- Detect anomalous behaviors.

Essentially there are three parts of a machine learning system: model, training, and inference. Figure 8-2 illustrates the high-level flow. At first, a machine learning model is created, and then it is trained with the training data. After training, the model would have "learned," based on the data, and is ready to be used for making useful prediction for new data, which is known as inference. It is worth mentioning that a large volume of data is required for the model to pick good rules and become reasonably accurate. In practice, the training of the model is a continuous process, bringing in new training data as we see more kinds of data from the real world, making the model predictions more accurate over time. Because of the iterations and amount of data that need to be processed, the training process is computationally intensive. The degree of computational requirement depends on the model (algorithm) being used and the size of the training database. The good news here is that once a model is trained, making an inference based on new data is fairly low cost.

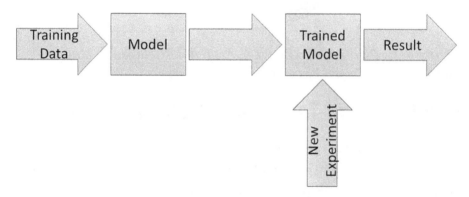

Figure 8-2. *Representation of a Machine Learning System*

Models

A machine learning (ML) model is fundamentally a recipe (i.e., statistical representation of the system) learned using examples (i.e., training data) with an ability to predict behavior given new data. In other words, a machine learning model is fundamentally the representation of a learning system that can be used to predict (i.e., infer) results for new data.

The processes machines use to learn are known as algorithms. Different algorithms learn in different ways. With the right model, as new data is provided to the "machine," the algorithm's performance improves, thereby resulting in increasing "intelligence" over time.

Training

Training refers to the model being fed with the data such that it learns the rules or improves the model. The structure of the data will be different depending upon the type of machine learning and the chosen model. Data points are generally represented as a feature vector, or feature. Each feature represents one attribute of the data. A vector is just like an array data structure, discussed previously.

So, taking an example, let's say we are designing a machine learning system to predict the price of a car in resale. The actual prices of cars sold previously, along with the descriptions of cars, will be fed to the learning model. The car description will have multiple attributes (features) like maker of the car, age of the car, the distance the car has been driven, and so on. Each of these features can be represented using one of the following types of data:

1. Categorical Data: Data that takes one of the few values in a set, for example, color of a car

2. Binary Data: Data that has two values, for example, whether a car has valid insurance or not

3. Numerical Data: Data that is a number, for example, price of a car

4. Graphical Data: Data that is in graphical form, for example, picture of a car

As part of the training process, we usually divide the available data for training into parts: one part used for training and learning and the other part used for validation/checking accuracy of the model. Given a trained model, we're ready for inference. As mentioned in the preceding, we're never really done training, as we need to constantly update our training data set to accurately reflect the real-world data we encounter using the model.

Prediction (Inference)

Now, once the model is ready and trained, the "trained model" is used for "prediction" or more formally "inference" with new data. The model is fed the new data and predicts the "result/output" for the same. From the computation resource perspective, inference is much faster than training because it can be done in real time or near real time in many cases.

Categories of Machine learning

In the context of machine learning, there are some well-known categories of learning problems. The key ones are (1) supervised, (2) unsupervised, (3) semi-supervised, and (4) reinforcement learning.

Supervised Learning

We know that in machine learning, we feed data to a model and the model learns using the data. In the case of supervised learning, the data is labeled with the right answer (we know what is good and what is bad, if you will). So, essentially, the model is being supervised while training. Another way to look at it is a person curating the data and creating the (good/bad) labels, essentially supervising the model. Supervised learning models the relationship between the output and the input data such that it can predict the output values for new data based on the derived (learned) relationships from the previous data sets. In other words, supervised learning can be considered a form of function approximation. Supervised learning is the most common machine learning technique applied in real-life use cases.

One example is when we are creating a spam detector engine. The model is fed with the description of the message along with the label (spam or "not a spam"). The learning is anchored around the label that is the correct answer (as per the supervisor). There are two major subcategories of supervised learning:

1.   Regression: The simplest form of regression is linear regression where we attempt to fit a straight line to a given set of data. In more complex regression systems, the predicted value (output) will fall within a continuous spectrum (it won't be a binary value like true or false). An example of a regression system is a car/house price predictor that will be used to predict the price of a given car/house based on the description of the same.

2.   Classification: In a classification system, the prediction falls in one of a few classes (also referred to as groupings or clusters). An example of a classification system would be a spam detector that will classify whether or not a given message is spam.

In supervised learning, there are many algorithms that can be used, some of the most common ones being

- Linear regression

- Logistic regression

- Nearest neighbor

- Naïve Bayes

- Decision trees

- Support vector machines

Unsupervised Learning

In contrast to supervised learning, with unsupervised learning, the model studies data to identify clusters, segmentation, and patterns. In this case, the data fed to the learning model is unlabeled. Essentially, that means there is no right or wrong answer key to the data set. The machine determines correlations and relationships by learning from the available data. This is pretty easy to do visually in two or even three dimensions, but as you can imagine, it is not intuitive with more dimensions, where each feature is a new dimension. A couple of applications of unsupervised learning are anomaly detection and categorizing similar objects. Again, there are many algorithms that can be used for unsupervised learning; however, the most common ones are

- K-means clustering

- Association rules

Semi-supervised Learning

Semi-supervised learning is used to address similar problems as supervised learning. It combines the techniques from both supervised and unsupervised learning. In semi-supervised learning, the machine is provided some labeled data, along with additional data that is not labeled. Typical use cases will be image and speech analysis, web content classification, protein sequence classification, and so on.

Reinforcement Learning

A reinforcement learning algorithm continuously learns from the environment in an iterative fashion. In the process, the model learns from the experiences of the environment. In other words, in reinforcement learning, the model is provided a set of allowed actions, rules, and potential outcomes (rewards). Essentially, the rules of the game are defined. The model then applies the rules and takes one of many possible actions and earns a reward. Based on the reward (outcome), the model determines what series of actions will lead to an optimal or optimized result. Reinforcement learning is how we learn to play a game and get better. The rules and objectives are clearly defined. However, the outcome depends on the judgment of the player who must adjust the approach in response to the environment, skill, and actions of the other player.

Machine Learning in Practice

Machine learning is prevalent in all aspects of life today. For example, social media platforms use machine learning for face detection, image recognition, automatic friend suggestion, and so on. Ecommerce and other product/service providers use machine learning for personalized recommendations. Virtual personal assistants use machine learning for speech recognition, natural language processing, and conversations. Self-driving cars use machine learning for navigation and controls. In the financial world, banks, for example, use machine learning to predict loan defaults and accordingly approve/reject/limit loan applications. Also, financial institutions use machine learning to detect fraudulent transactions. These are just a few examples to illustrate the wide and growing usage in day-to-day life; there are many more.

Leading Machine Learning Frameworks

The rapid advancements in the machine learning world have led to proliferation of frameworks. One of the most common frameworks today is TensorFlow. TensorFlow is an open source platform for machine learning. Because of its comprehensive toolset, it enables the creation, training, and use of machine learning models easily. There are many other frameworks like Microsoft Cognitive Toolkit (CNTK), Theano, Scikit Learn, Caffe, H2O, Amazon Machine Learning, Torch, Google Cloud ML Engine, Azure ML Studio, Spark MLlib, and MXNet, for instance. Some of these frameworks are better suited to specific areas or applications of machine learning than others. Interested readers can find more about any of these frameworks, but any further discussion of them is beyond the scope of this book.

To make it easy to use the machine learning frameworks, higher-level APIs are created, which support multiple frameworks and also abstract the framework differences. For example, Keras, developed by Google, is an open source software library that provides a Python interface for artificial neural networks. It works on Linux and OS X and supports multiple back ends including TensorFlow. Another parallel high-level API is PyTorch. PyTorch was developed by Facebook and works across Windows, Linux, and OS X.

Machine Learning and Cloud Computing

We often hear machine learning and "cloud" discussed together. A casual observer might think they are connected somehow. Theoretically speaking, they are not. Cloud computing is about computing resources being available at will, and machine learning is about making computers learn and make use of that learning. The reason we often talk about them together is because machine learning training usually requires a lot of computing resources. Therefore, it makes good sense to leverage cloud computing for procuring and using these resources. As machine learning assumes increase in importance in business applications, there is a strong possibility of this technology being offered as a cloud-based service known as Machine Learning as a Service (MLaaS).

The Way Forward

Artificial intelligence/machine learning (AI/ML) has the potential to touch literally all aspects of our lives. By the time we read or reread this section, any specific estimates on deployments and proliferation of AI and ML across solutions will be out of date. As per Gartner, "Artificial Intelligence and Machine Learning have reached a critical tipping point and will increasingly augment and extend virtually every technology enabled service, thing, or application."[3] One thing for sure, AI/ML is making inroads and making real impact. As it progresses and more businesses look to leverage the capabilities and benefits, ML will become an integral part of intelligent systems.

We have reached or maybe exceeded human-level performance at narrowly defined tasks such as strategy games, visual image detection, and parsing natural language.

There is a lot of debate around how things will shape up around machine learning. As we can imagine, with the continuous improvement in computation capability, data storage, processing, and learning, machines will continue to become more and more intelligent and powerful.

Extrapolating the advancements, some imagine that in the foreseeable future, machines could be capable of having "artificial general intelligence," a more recent term. Artificial general intelligence is the intelligence of a machine that has the capacity to understand/learn any intellectual task that a human can. Today, it is a primary goal of some focused AI research to gain the artificial general intelligence level where complete problems are modeled and solutions are hypothesized. Applications include computer vision, natural language understanding, and dealing with unexpected circumstances for solving real-world problems.

---

[3]Kasey Panetta, "Gartner's Top 10 Strategic Technology Trends for 2017," October 18, 2016, www.gartner.com/smarterwithgartner/gartners-top-10-technology-trends-2017/.

Whether or not machines reach the "artificial general intelligence" level, machine learning is going to help solve problems that are intractable today. For instance, machine learning can help discover what genes are involved in specific disease pathways. Based on this, machine learning can be used to determine the most effective personalized treatment based on patient DNA and other related characteristics. Additionally, machine learning is enabling autonomous driving and will continue to improve safety. There are plenty of studies extrapolating the benefits of autonomous driving saving lives resulting from accident avoidance and so on.

Like any technology, there are potentially negative side effects of advancements in machine learning. Some worry about machines taking over humans. While that may sound futuristic, there are more immediate challenges or concerns. For instance, machine learning models may sound like black boxes. While a lot of time can be spent in validating the model, one can never be sure about the output of the machine learning model (especially deep learning). Incorrect results could be incredibly costly or even fatal.

There are potentially dire consequences of machine learning, some of which Elon Musk and Stephen Hawking present. For example, Musk has repeatedly warned that AI will soon become just as smart as humans and said that when it does, we should all be scared because humanity's very existence is at stake. Hawking said the emergence of artificial intelligence could be the "worst event in the history of our civilization."[4] And he followed up saying, "The development of full artificial intelligence could spell the end of the human race." And then there are others like James Barat who have termed machine learning as "our final invention" with his

---

[4]www.usatoday.com/story/tech/talkingtech/2017/11/07/hawking-ai-could-worst-event-history-our-civilization/839298001/.

book *Our Final Invention: Artificial Intelligence and the End of the Human Era*.[5] The book discusses the potential benefits and possible risks of human-level or superhuman artificial intelligence

A fundamental misunderstanding or maybe myth is that AI/ML is the solution for all the problems. Some of us feel like the AI/ML systems train themselves and become the solution for everything. The reality is that in order for a system to do something as simple as distinguish a cat from a dog, it must undergo supervised (deep) learning with volumes of data where its neural networks are trained to distinguish one from the other. So, while machine learning may sound like a potential replacement for an existing technology, we must be mindful of the time, effort, and resources it takes to model, train, and use a machine learning model. For example, machine learning may sound like the technology to replace traditional statistical analysis algorithms; however, knowing the time and resource penalty to build accurate models, we would be better off using the conventional statistical algorithms in most cases. As we've learned in previous chapters, we should be using "the" most appropriate tool for that specific use case.

Summary

In this chapter, we started with the fundamentals of machine learning, their benefits, and the evolution of machine learning. Then we talked about the various types of machine learning and the connection of machine learning with cloud computing. We followed that up with how machine learning is looking to shape up in the future.

---

[5]Thomas Dunne Books, 2013.

References

- Artificial Intelligence/Machine Learning Primer: www.actiac.org/system/files/Artificial%20 Intelligence%20Machine%20Learning%20Primer.pdf

- Machine Learning for All: www.coursera.org/learn/ uol-machine-learning-for-all

- Machine Learning: www.coursera.org/learn/ machine-learning

APPENDIX A

Software Development Lifecycle

Whether you are working on a one-person project or as part of a complex multitiered project with multiple teams, you should understand the software development lifecycle. Each phase of the lifecycle has a purpose that will help you write better software. The following phases can be applied to both agile and waterfall project management practices (Figure A-1). The waterfall method is the method where each phase is completed before the work on the next phase begins, like a pool of water that fills up and then spills over falling into the next pool. The agile or iterative method is where software is developed partially, evaluated, and then incrementally adjusted until it is sufficient. This is considered agile because at each iteration the project can change direction to better serve the users; in the waterfall method, the project would have to start over from the beginning. The formality of the artifacts and collateral that are produced by each phase will vary by industry and requirements of the projects you may find yourself working on. It is also important to remember that these phases are not strictly linear. You may find that you do some planning, some analysis, and some design before completing any one of those phases. Equally important is to remember that every software project is different and these lifecycle stages are guidelines.

© Paul D. Crutcher, Neeraj Kumar Singh, and Peter Tiegs 2021
P. D. Crutcher et al., *Essential Computer Science*,
https://doi.org/10.1007/978-1-4842-7107-0

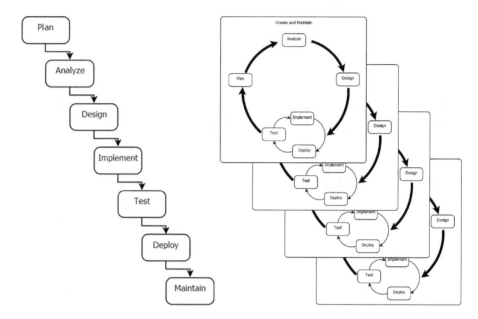

Figure A-1. *Software Development Lifecycle Phases*

Planning

The planning phase is used to determine what software you will create. In planning, you think about what you want the software to do and begin thinking about how you want to do the implementation. Once you have some coherent thoughts on this, start writing those thoughts down. Planning is important for all software development projects, even those using agile methodologies. The detail and length of planning should be determined by the amount of formality needed by the software and/or the industry the software is being targeted to. For instance, planning on an agile project may occur briefly to define what a minimal viable product (MVP) should be for a given iteration. Likewise, on a project for a medical imaging device, much more detailed and rigorous planning may be required.

One important point about planning is that the original plan is rarely what the result will be. It is impossible to predict the future, and plan for every possible change that will affect the plan. There is certainly a point of diminishing returns on planning. Planning will not reveal every possible thing that could occur for your project, nor will everything in the plan materialize. The key to planning is understanding the project and then adjusting to the things that happen in later stages of the lifecycle, without breaking.

Analysis

In the analysis phase, you will define use cases and decompose the problem into logical blocks to help you understand the system, to the best of your ability. Use cases help you focus on how the software will be used; this helps define what the software does and what the users need and prevents creating software that will not be useful. In this phase, you would compare possible algorithms for use in you project, leveraging Big-Oh analysis. This is where you should also develop an understanding of the type and amount of data that your program will be processing. During the analysis phase, you should consider any constraints such as security requirements, usability, cost, feature trade-offs, and long-term support. For instance, if your software will be used over a network, the analysis phase is when you should analyze the network throughput, latency, and frequency requirements for your solution.

The analysis phase may include creating prototypes to better understand the problem. It is important to remember that this is not the implantation phase. Prototypes should be used to understand the problem better and how to approach it. The code that is written as prototypes may not (and probably should not) be included in the implementations.

Architecture and Design

The design of the software is how all the various parts fit together into a consistent whole solution to the problem. Typically we build a solution architecture that lays out the components of a software and how/where they interact. There are at least two interaction areas to cover during the architecture and design phase. First is defining how people will interact with the solution. Second is defining the application programming interfaces (APIs) that define how the components interact with each other. Some software may not have a significant human interaction component, but all software will need to define interfaces (APIs) for access and control.

It's a good idea to do user interface mockups during this phase, to show how a user will interact with the system. If the software is sufficiently complex, various diagrams should be created to help fully understand the design of the software so it can be implemented. A block or object diagram can show how the various components in the software are related to each other. A sequence diagram can show the order that the components communicate with each other and how they interact with each other. A "paper" prototype, mockups, or wireframe diagrams can show what a user might see as they interact with the software. Finally, an API spec should be defined during the design phase to clearly communicate how to interact with the software. The API spec is a key output of the design phase, and it can act as a contract between the components.

Implementation

The implementation phase is where you actually write the software that will address the problems you are trying to solve. You should already have a plan for the implementation and have analyzed the problem to understand the data and algorithms you need. Don't jump into implementation, even on an agile project, without at least some thought and discussion on the architecture and design. It is, of course, possible to jump straight into implementation, and for the simplest of solutions, that might be ok. But even simple projects will benefit from a lightweight application of planning, analysis, and design.

The technologies and programing languages for your implementation may already be determined for you as constraints of the environment or business. If not, use what you learned in the analysis phase to choose your technology stack.

Test

Testing your software is important to demonstrate that you have indeed solved the problem (verification) and that you have not introduced any new problems or so-called "bugs" (validation).

With the practice of test-driven development (TDD), the test phase and the implementation phase are combined. In TDD, a test is written that will fail until the software is implemented to pass the test. Then the next test and the next part of the implementation are created and so on. More commonly tests are created after the implementation is complete.

Most tests should be written so that they can be run automatically. There is likely some level of testing that cannot be easily automated. These tests should still be documented like a checklist so that the procedure to run these tests can be repeated.

The goals of testing are to discover errors in the software that can have adverse effects on users and data, for instance. Testing can also prove that the software does what is expected. Coverage is a concept in testing that measures how much of the software is covered during testing. Only the simplest of software can have every possible input tested, so coverage helps us discuss how much of the software is tested, which can help build confidence that the software is valid. There are different types of coverage metrics we can measure to indicate how much of the software is covered.

The most common coverage measurement is line coverage. Line coverage measures how many lines or statements of the software are executed during testing. Another common coverage measurement is branch coverage, which measures how many paths through the code are covered.

Test results and coverage measurements provide us with a sense of assurance that the software we develop will work for the users of the software.

Deploy

The deployment phase is when the software is made available for use. There are many types of software deployment. For boxed software deployment, it is preparing the final (compiled) software for inclusion with installer software on a disk. With the growth of the Internet, this mechanism for deployment is not very common anymore. More commonly new deployments are available for download from the Internet, either through an application store or as OS- and language-specific packages. It should also be noted that a lot of software that is written today is never distributed publicly; it's used inside of companies to automate and/or solve specific business problems.

Not only are there many methods to deploy software; software gets deployed in a variety of cadences. Some software is deployed multiple times a day, some once a year, and some only once. Despite the variety of deployment mechanisms and cadences, there are common things you should be aware of when deploying software, such as software licensing, virus scans, and security checks.

The first key to deployment is to understand what audience or audiences you are targeting. This will determine the type of packaging or installer you need to prepare. Once you know your packaging format, consider automating the mechanism of delivering the package of software to your audience. The second key to deployment to consider is a checklist of actions that need to be completed before deployment. These actions should include items such as making sure whatever license you release your software under matches the license of the ingredient software used in the making of your solution. Of course, you should verify that your tests have run and are successful. The checklist you define will depend on what your audience needs or desires.

Much like testing and test-driven development, continuous integration and continuous deployment (CI/CD) brings deployment into the implementation phase.

Maintenance

Last but certainly not least is the maintenance phase. This is when you change the software to maintain over time. Maintaining software is a much more common activity than creating new software. While maintaining software, you need to be able to identify what parts of the source code need to change (analyze), make changes (design and implementation), test those changes (test), and deploy the new version of the software (deploy). At times, especially when dealing with software that you did not write, this can be difficult. There are some simple actions you can take in other phases to simplify the maintenance phase. In the design phase, you can design the blocks to have very clear, singular purposes. You can also make sure that certain behaviors are only in one block of software. In the implementation phase, you can follow the design as best as possible. Also, during the implementation, comment your code with information about what you are doing and why you are doing it. Consider these comments as a letter to a future maintainer. Having automated tests from the test phase can help prove that any changes during maintenance have not created new issues.

The software development lifecycle for your project will be unique, whether it is closer to the waterfall model, highly iterative, or something in between. This framework of phases should help you manage a broader set of activities, beyond just writing the code.

Software Engineering Practices

There are many practices for the various phases and types of software development beyond writing the code. Here we will cover some common software engineering practices, including tools and techniques that you can apply to your software project.

Planning and Management Practices: Agile

Agile practices, practices that attempt to follow the guidance of the Agile Manifesto (https://agilemanifesto.org/), have become a dominant approach to software development. Agile practices start with the concept of a minimal viable product or MVP. The MVP is a version of software that provides the minimum capabilities for users to use and developers to learn from.

Scrum

Scrum is one of the most common agile practices for organizing work. In a nutshell, the scrum practice is focused on the short daily scrum meeting like a rugby scrum, or American football huddle. In the scrum or huddle, the team coordinates on the work for the day and then breaks out and does the work.

The work that the team needs to do is divided into small completable segments, called stories. Those stories are organized into an ordered list called a backlog. The ordered list of stories is then divided into groups that a scrum team can complete in a fixed time segment. This time segment can be any length, but at the end of each time segment, there should be a viable/usable software. The time segments are called sprints or iterations. They are called sprints to remind the team that they are short and will finish. They are called iterations because after one is complete, small adjustments can be made and then you start again. These iterations commonly range from one week to one month, with two weeks being the most common.

Scum recommends three ceremonies in addition to the scrum or huddle. First, before the beginning of each iteration, the team confirms what stories the team will be completing in that iteration. The team will use the ordered backlog and, if available, feedback from previous iterations to determine what should be done to have a viable/usable software product at the end of the sprint. This is called the planning ceremony. The second ceremony scrum recommends is the review. This happens at the end of the sprint and is where the team reviews the software that they created with their stakeholders and users of the software, if that is possible. Any feedback from the review should be added to the backlog and taken into consideration for future iterations. A retrospective, also conducted at the end of a sprint, is the third ceremony. In the retrospective, the team examines how they are working and looks for areas to improve. Any feedback the team has will again be used to plan future iterations.

Scrum also recommends three roles to coordinate the work. The most important role is the team. The team is all the developers in the scrum. Next is the product owner or PO. The product owner's main responsibility is to represent the stakeholders for the team and manage the backlog of work. Finally, there is the coach; this person's responsibility is to enable the team to work effectively. The coach will organize the ceremonies and help the team implement any of the feedback from the retrospectives. The coach was previously referred to as the scrum master, but that term has fallen out of favor.

While scrum can be effective and is often a developer's first introduction to agile practices, there are some constraints to the practice. First, scrum does not specifically outline how the work is broken into stories. It does not cover requirements, analysis, or design; in some ways, it assumes that those are already complete. Second, scrum does not cover how the work will be implemented, validated, or deployed. There are other agile practices that cover these areas such as test-driven development, paired programming, and continuous integration and deployment (CI/CD). Third, scrum works a specific team size of from five to nine people. Fewer people than that, and all of the ceremonies are not really required; more people than that, and the ceremonies are not sufficient.

Kanban

Kanban is another agile practice for organizing work. The Kanban process was originally developed by Toyota in Japan for automotive manufacturing. Kanban means a signboard in Japanese. The original Kanban practice used a card or sign that traveled with the work until the work was completed; then the card was returned to the board. If no cards were available on the board, then work was stalled somewhere in the process, and the team could focus on that area until work was completed and a card returned. Cards were intentionally limited to reduce the amount of uncompleted work in progress. For agile software, this principle of WIP (work in progress) limits can be applied to the development of software. An individual or team can have a WIP limit and start work up to that point and then focus on completing that work.

Kanban is like scrum in that work is organized into small compliable segments and then organized into a backlog. Also, like scrum, Kanban does not cover how work will be implemented, validated, or deployed.

Kanban differs from scrum in that instead of fixed time segments like iterations, it has a fixed amount of work in progress. Kanban works well when the work items are of similar scale. Kanban can also scale down to a smaller team size or even an individual. It can scale down because Kanban does not have the concepts of the various scrum ceremonies or dedicated roles.

Analysis and Design

As noted in the preceding, neither scrum nor Kanban specifically covers the analysis and design phases of a project. This has led to the incorrect belief that analysis, architecture, and design are not needed for agile projects. Instead, those practices assume that analysis, architecture, and design have happened to create the backlog. If that is not the case, then you might consider inserting this work as work items or stories into the backlog and have that work as part of the regular work the team does. Another approach is having dedicated time periods such as every third sprint to analyze and design the upcoming work to load into the backlog. Another approach that could work with a larger team is to have one team responsible for doing the analysis and design and feeding the backlog through their own agile processes.

Scaling Agile Practices

Both the practices of scrum and Kanban work well for small teams; however, those practices become problematic as the number of people on the team and the number of teams working on the project scale up. There are a few recommendations about how to approach scaling up agile practices such as Scrum of Scrums or the Scaled Agile Framework (SAFe). The key to scaling agile practices up is to constantly keep agility in mind – being able to quickly change direction and get back up to speed.

Documentation

Documenting your software project is an important way to communicate to the future. In the future, there may be different developers or maintainers of the software. Ideally there will be future users of the software. Questions such as why does it work this way or how do I do this should be found in the documentation, without direct contact to you or the development team.

Requirements, Design, and Architecture

Documenting the requirements, the design, and the architecture is a way to record and communicate what you learned during the design and analysis phases. This is to inform the developer(s) on what to develop.

The formality of writing requirements and design will vary by the type and scope of projects. This formality could be as informal as writing a user story in the form "A user desires some outcome, because of some reason." A fully specified safety-centric software system where every known possibility is documented will require more formality in its requirements.

We find that for most projects, using the Cockburn use case template is a highly effective way of capturing and communicating the requirements. The template helps to guide the requirement creation, and it helps avoid specifying design and implementation details into the requirement.

Implementation details, like how to interface with a system and what components make up a system, can be documented in the design and architecture. Design and architecture will typically have illustrations in addition to text. These documents should inform the developers of the project how the software should work within itself and with the world.

Over time the requirements will change, the design will grow, and the architecture will morph. It is important to remember that these documents should also be able to change via controlled practices.

Comments and Code

The code itself is a document about what is implemented. Comments in the code should be limited to adding context and not a retelling of what is in the code. This context will be helpful to maintainers of the code.

Well-written code is code that acts as its own documentation. Meaningful variable and function names can help code be its own documentation. However, source code is limited in expressiveness compared to natural languages. When this additional expressiveness is needed, it is a good time to write additional comments around that code.

User

User documentation can take multiple forms: web pages, online help, or even console output. This documentation should provide a road map to your software and guide the users to accomplish what they desire.

Testing

Testing your software is done to both validate and verify your software. Verification is proving that your software behaves as expected, and validation is proving that your software does not behave in unexpected ways.

Phases and Categories of Testing and Goals

Testing your software can be done with various goals and at different phases of the software lifecycle.

Algorithm Testing, Unit Testing, Integration Testing, and the Like

Algorithm testing is typically done early in the lifecycle. Algorithm testing is used to test a selected algorithm with a sample data set that your software will be using. This is used to profile and understand whether the algorithm will be the best match for the data.

Unit testing is done throughout the development of the software. It is often tied into the continuous integration system. Continuous integration is the practice of building and testing your software on every commit to an SCM (source control management) system, which we discuss in more detail in this chapter. Unit testing is when you test the software at the smallest unit possible. This could be a single function, or class in object-oriented programming. The goal of unit testing is to validate the units of software work with a variety of inputs. Having unit tests with sufficient coverage is helpful during the maintenance phase, because it allows a unit of software to be improved while demonstrating that the inputs and outputs are not negatively changed.

If unit testing is focused on individual software units, then integration testing is focused on testing how those units work together. Integration testing has a primary goal of verifying that the software does what it is expected to do when all of the pieces come together. It also has a validation role in that it will help identify any adverse interactions between various units of the software.

There are other types of testing to be aware of, such as exploratory testing, performance testing, and user acceptance testing. Exploratory testing is where a user specifically "explores" to find issues that have not been found through the other types of testing that are done regularly. Performance testing is looking to record the performance in time or memory of your software. User acceptance testing is testing whether a user will accept the software deliverable.

Test-Driven Development

Test-driven development (TDD) is the discipline of developing your tests first, before you write any of the production code, and then writing the production code to make the tests pass. This is a particularly useful practice, especially for unit tests. It can keep the test coverage high for your software. It can also help enforce a good modular design, by making it difficult to have cross-dependencies given the goal of always having to pass tests. Despite all these benefits, it is not practiced as much as it could be. TDD requires a fairly complete knowledge of what the software should do, which is not always possible. It also is sometimes difficult to get over the hurdle of writing the tests first when the value to the users comes from the production software, trading the immediate satisfaction of writing the production code first to the delayed satisfaction of writing tests first.

Developing for Debug

Debugging is typically the exploration of the software to find the root cause of a defect or bug in the software. A debugger is software that will allow a developer to step through the code, one line at a time. This brings the computer speed down to the speed of the developer, so they can observe the effects of each line being executed. For source line debugging, it is best to have the source code available when you are debugging the software. If you do not have the source code, debug symbols are the next best thing. Debug symbols provide source-level information to a debugger without providing the full source code. There are situations where developers will need to debug without the benefit of source code or symbols. When you are developing software, there are activities you can do to support debug for the future engineers needing to debug your software.

Asserts and Exceptions

Asserts and exceptions are program language constructs that can be used to support debugging. An assertion will act as a checkpoint on some fact in the source code, like the value of a variable. An assertion is typically implemented with an assert keyword, which will typically stop the execution of the software, if the assertion is false. Adding assertions to your code will help prove that the data you expect is available. Assertions are typically automatically removed when the code is compiled in an optimization. And assertions that evaluate false actually halt the program, so assertions should be used with caution.

Exceptions are like assertions. Exceptions will check for an event that is not expected to occur. When an exception occurs, an exception handler in your code can catch the exception. Once an exception is caught, it can be raised up the stack for another exception handler to deal with, or it can be handled immediately. A raised exception will provide data about where a defect originates from. For debugging, unhandled exceptions are defects that need to be addressed. Adding code to raise exceptions is a good technique for making your code more debugger-friendly.

Logging and Tracing

Two other practices that help make your code more debugger-friendly are logging and tracing. Logging is recording events that occur in the software to an external file, for instance, so a human or machine can go back and follow the events of software execution. Tracing is using logs or live data to observe the behavior of the software while it is running.

Most modern languages have built-in support for logging. It is a good practice to use these logging frameworks whenever possible. Using a logging framework will help distinguish between messages intended for the logs and messages intended for active users. When adding logging to your software, you need to strike a balance between how precise or frequent you want your log messages to be and the number of messages in the log. Remember that logging takes compute time and that if there is too much information in the log, it may hide meaningful events.

Source Control Management

Source control management (SCM) is the practice of managing the source code of your software. This practice includes managing the directory structure of the source code, maintaining a history of revisions of the code, and versioning the code.

Purpose and Mechanism

Source code management gives the developer or development team confidence to proceed with development knowing that they can go back to a previous revision of the source code, should they need too. A fundamental purpose of SCM is to preserve the progression of the source code development.

SCM systems allow for branches of the software to exist simultaneously, so different revisions of source code can be compared or merged. This allows a team of developers to operate safely, in their own environment, without impacting each other with moment-to-moment changes. When your code branch is ready, you use SCM to integrate the branch to a trunk or mainline of the source code.

SCM systems typically have the same common concepts (Table B-1), although different tools may call these concepts by different terms.

Table B-1. *Common SCM Terms*

Term	Definition
Workspace	The directory structure on a development machine for the source code of software.
Revision	A single incremental change of the source code.
Branch	A line of revisions that are derived from a single point in the past.
Mainline	The branch of the code that is where the integration of various branches occurs. Sometimes called trunk.
Version	A specific revision that has meaning or value.

Imagine using SCM for a small team. For example, a developer will check out a workspace. The workspace will define the directory structure of the source code on the developer's system. As the developer makes changes to the source code, they will commit this code to the SCM system creating a revision. The developer may be creating multiple revisions on a branch. They will then want to share their revisions with the rest of the team by merging their revisions into the mainline. On the mainline, the development team will define the next version by linearly selecting the head revision on the mainline.

For another example, a bug is discovered in the recent version and needs to be fixed. In this case, a developer will check out a workspace based on that previous version. Then they will create a branch to fix the code. As they fix the code, the developer will create revisions by progressively committing their code to the SCM system. They can compare their revisions to the revisions on another branch to identify changes or even to help discover the root cause of the bug. Once they have fixed the bug, they can again merge into the mainline and create another version.

Both examples are somewhat simplified and mix concepts from multiple SCM tools. Each SCM tool will have its own process and workflow. SCM tools can generally be split into two categories: centralized and distributed. A centralized SCM system maintains in a single location a definitive list of revisions and versions. This has an advantage of maintaining linearity of the software and explicit control of a version. A distributed SCM system does not require a central system to maintain the distributions but allows multiple systems to maintain individual history and then add history of revisions from another node in the SCM system. This has the advantage of allowing the full capabilities of an SCM system while being disconnected from the team, but the linearity of the revisions is not guaranteed.

Tools

There are many source code management tools. Each tool has its own unique differences. In the following, we will review two of the most common tools that demonstrate the centralized and distributed SCM systems.

Perforce Helix

Perforce Helix is a good example of a centralized version control system for SCM. It allows developers to define their workspace from the various branches in the overall source code tree. By being a centralized system, it can enforce that revisions are committed in a linear order and can maintain that order. One area where Perforce Helix stands out is how it handles source assets that are not text, such as large binary files like game assets.

Git

Git has become the industry de facto SCM. It is an example of a distributed revision control system. Git maintains a repository history of revisions locally within the workspace. To interact with another instance of the Git repository, a developer can push changes to the other instance or pull and merge changes from that other instance. Because Git does not have a centralized location, other solutions like GitHub have been put in place to act as a central instance of the repository. Other processes have emerged around Git to help define definitive versions such as having merge or pull request as a gate to a mainline branch and using tags to capture the linear progression for versions.

Build Optimizations and Tools

Build tools coordinate the compilation and linking of the source code into usable software.

Purpose and Mechanism

Originally source code had to be first compiled into object files one at a time, and then all those object files had to be linked together into an executable or library. As software got larger and larger, a tool to coordinate the effort of compiling and linking many files together became necessary. This is the basis of what a build tool does.

Adding to the complexity of compiling source code into object files, some of those object files depended on other object files to exist before they could be linked together. And in this case, some of those upstream object files were needed for more than one downstream object file. Managing this collection of object file dependencies is another piece of what the build tool does. Build tools will typically enable a declaration of dependencies and will make sure that the dependencies are satisfied before attempting to compile and link a file. Most build tools will optimize the satisfaction of dependencies by first checking if they exist and then creating them only once, if it does not exist.

Scripted or interpreted languages like Python, Ruby, and JavaScript don't need to compile the source code into object files. Scripted languages can still benefit from build tools that manage the dependencies and create packages and other collateral.

Another thing a build tool does is manage configuration parameters for multiple configurations to inform the compiler and linker how to behave. This allows the object files and software to have multiple configurations, such as debug instances or even support for multiple operating system instances.

This ability to coordinate multiple tools like a compiler and a linker led build tools to be used to coordinate additional tools that are expected in a modern software project like unit test runners, security checkers, and document generators.

Build tools will typically have their own source file to define the configurations and parameters. The configuration file will usually list targets that will be the output of some action and the dependencies that need to be satisfied before the output can be created. Typically build tools also allow a developer to define the tools and parameters to call to create the output. Make and most modern build tools also have default rules for doing the basics of compiling and linking object files.

Tools

There are a lot of build tools available. Some are specific to a language, and many modern languages such as Go and Rust have a build tool distributed with the language. Some build tools are fully declarative, meaning that all the possible options and dependencies are defined in the configuration files. Most build tools are primarily declarative with limited scripting ability for loops and conditional statements. Another category of build tools are generators, like Cmake and GNU Autotools, which use data to configure and generate a build script. Then this build script can be called by another build tool.

Make

Make is one of the older build tools. There are multiple implementations of make that have mostly the same feature set; the most common make is GNU make. The make configuration file is called the Makefile. Make provides a declarative syntax for defining targets and dependencies. Each target line starts with the target followed by a space-separated list of dependencies on a single line. The commands to create the target are the subsequent lines, tab indented, under the target line. Typically, these lines are shell commands that make use of the underlying command shell. By default, the targets are expected to be files that are created on the file system; however, a target can have a `.phony` decorator added to it so that make knows the target can be satisfied even if no output file is created. This allows for an easy name like ALL or drivers to be applied to a list of dependencies instead of the direct output, such as `my_cool_program.exe`.

Gradle

Gradle is a more modern build tool that is built on top of the Groovy language and its Java Virtual Machine (JVM). Gradle configurations are written in a domain-specific language designed for builds. Like make, Gradle can define targets and dependencies. Unlike make, these targets do not have to be files that are created. Gradle remembers what targets have been satisfied in a build cache. Gradle can even share this build cache between multiple systems on a network making it easier to split the build work to improve build time. The commands to satisfy the targets do not have to be shell commands; they can be methods in Groovy.

Cmake and Ninja

Cmake takes a different approach than Gradle or make. Instead of defining the build targets and commands directly in the CMakefile, Cmake defines a script for generating the targets and commands for another build tool. This provides the ability to consistently model the targets and dependencies for your software project and then generate equivalent logic for multiple systems, such as different integrated development environments or different implementations of make.

Ninja is a modern build tool like make. It is intended to be highly performant and minimal compared to build systems like Gradle. Cmake generates Ninja build files, a common practice, with the rich syntax being handled by Cmake and the performant build done by Ninja.

Continuous Integration and Continuous Delivery

Continuous integration (CI) is the practice of building and testing your software on every commit to an SCM system. Continuous delivery builds on the concept of continuous integration to deliver the software to users automatically, typically when the software is merged to the mainline in the SCM system. The term continuous integration was coined by Martin Fowler in 2000.

Purpose and Mechanism

Prior to the practice of continuous integration, when a new version of the software needed to be built and tested, all the various branches and different developers' work would come together for integration in a so-called "big-bang." A build would be attempted, and if not successful, engineers would have to find the reasons. This could be caused by code conflict or even incompatible code between engineers. Once the initial work to resolve the conflicts and any side effects would be resolved and the build be complete, then testing could begin. All of this is very painful and time consuming, hence the moniker "big-bang." If this integration testing found issues, then the code needed to be changed and any side effects again resolved, and the process would start again. Historically this process could take days or even weeks. So we want to avoid big-bangs.

Continuous integration addresses this "big-bang" integration problem by shrinking integrations into a continuous stream of micro-integration events. In the practice of continuous integration, developers push their changes regularly, ideally daily, to be integrated to a mainline in the SCM system, using build tools that automatically build and validate (through unit testing, for instance) the new integrated version. If this build does not work, the developer can see that within hours and make corrections in the small amount of code that they worked on, instead of digging through everybody's code in the "big-bang" integration style. If the build is successful, then automated unit tests and integration tests can be run. Again, if the tests fail, there is only a small amount of code that could have introduced the failure, so the developer can easily find and fix their code.

Continuous integration systems wait for source code to be pushed to the SCM system and activate when there is a change. The CI system will either monitor the SCM system or be triggered by an event on the SCM system. At that point, the CI system will check out the code and invoke the build tool automatically, and then the CI system will run the tests. Typically, the CI system will report on the status of the build so the developer and the team can review the results.

Continuous deployment utilizes the same CI systems for deployment or delivery activities. After the source code is integrated, built, and tested, the CI system can be triggered to automatically deploy the software. The deployment may require additional steps or stages such as more testing, checking security scans, packaging the software for install, and copying it to a location to either run online or download to install on a local system.

Tools

Like build tools and SCM systems, there are a lot of options for CI/CD systems. They define the stages and steps to integrate and deploy the software. CI/CD systems also define how the tools will interact with the SCM systems.

Jenkins

Jenkins is one of the oldest CI/CD systems. It is still the most popular CI/ CD system. Jenkins provides a lot of flexibility in how it can be configured and deployed. Originally Jenkins enabled a wide variety of plugins to expand the configuration interface for defining the rules for your software's CI and CD. Jenkins also provides a scripted, domain-specific language and a declarative syntax, both based on Groovy, to define the CI/CD pipeline. Jenkins is typically installed on-premises, but there are online and commercial offerings. When Jenkins is installed on your premises, you need to provide your own compute capacity for build and testing.

CircleCI

CircleCI is a popular Software as a Service (SaaS) CI/CD system. It provides an online tool to create a CI/CD pipeline and the compute resources for compilation and testing. CircleCI provides a simple UI for defining the connection to the SCM system and a YAML-based declarative syntax for defining the pipeline.

GitLab CI/CD

GitLab CI/CD is an example of a CI/CD system that is built into the SCM system. The GitLab CI/CD system is available wherever the GitLab SCM system is installed. Because GitLab CI/CD is integrated with the SCM system, it requires minimal configuration to connect to the source code. For configuring the CI/CD pipeline, GitLab uses a YAML-based declarative syntax. Using the GitLab SaaS solution provides both the CI/CD system interface and the compute capacity for build and test. Using GitLab with your own environment requires you to provide your own compute capacity. Despite GitLab CI/CD being associated with the GitLab SCM solution, GitLab CI/CD can work with a variety of Git solutions including GitHub.

APPENDIX C

ACPI System States

Power optimization of computer systems has become very important. There are many governing bodies (like the California Energy Commission) that mandate a certain level of power efficiency in computing devices. In a computer system, there are multiple pieces of hardware and software that all need to be in sync. Therefore, a mechanism is needed for these pieces to pass information around. The Advanced Configuration and Power Interface Special Interest Group (ACPI SIG) developed such a standard, named after the group, ACPI.

ACPI provides an open standard that system firmware (BIOS) and operating systems use to discover, configure, and carry out system-specific operations. ACPI replaces the multiple earlier standards like Advanced Power Management (APM), MultiProcessor Specification, and the Plug and Play (PnP) BIOS Specification. ACPI defines a hardware abstraction interface across system firmware, computer hardware components, and operating systems. ACPI is the key element in operating system–directed configuration and power management (OSPM). In 2013, the ACPI SIG agreed to transfer the specification to the UEFI Forum, which now owns the specification.

ACPI defines standard operating states for systems, devices, and processors, among other things. Figure C-1 shows the various states defined by ACPI and transitions between them. In the following sections, we talk about these states and explain what they all mean.

© Paul D. Crutcher, Neeraj Kumar Singh, and Peter Tiegs 2021
P. D. Crutcher et al., *Essential Computer Science*,
https://doi.org/10.1007/978-1-4842-7107-0

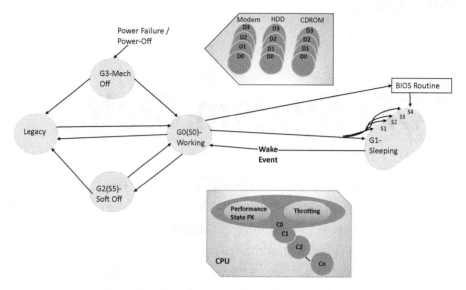

Figure C-1. *Global and System Power States and Transitions*

Global and System States

ACPI defines four global states and six system states. The global states are marked G0–G3, while the system states are marked as S0–S5. It must be noted, however, that some motherboard documents reference S6, which is not an ACPI-defined state. If you come across this, you can safely map this to G3.

ACPI defines a mechanism to transition the system between the working state (G0) and the sleeping state (G1) or the soft-off state (G2). During transitions between the working and sleeping states, the operating system will maintain your context, so you don't lose information on such transitions. ACPI defines the level of the G1 sleeping state by defining the system attributes of four types of ACPI sleeping states (S1, S2, S3, and S4). Each sleeping state is defined to allow implementations to trade-off cost, power, and wake latencies:

- G0/S0: In the G0 state, work is being performed by the OS/application software and the hardware. The CPU or any particular hardware device could be in any one of the defined power states (more on the device and CPU power states in a later section); however, some work will be taking place in the system.

  a. S0: System is in a fully working state.

- G1: In the G1 state, the system is assumed to be doing no work. Prior to entering the G1 state, OSPM will place devices in a device power state compatible with the system sleeping state to be entered; if a device is enabled to wake the system, then OSPM will place these devices into the lowest Dx state from which the device supports wake.

  a. S1: The S1 state is defined as a low wake latency sleeping state. In this state, the entire system context is preserved with the exception of CPU caches. Before entering S1, OSPM will flush the system caches.

  b. S2: The S2 state is defined as a low wake latency sleep state. This state is similar to the S1 sleeping state where any context except for system memory may be lost.

  c. S3: Commonly referred to as Standby, Sleep, or Suspend to RAM (STR). The S3 state is defined as a low wake latency sleep state. From the software viewpoint, this state is functionally the same as the S2 state. The operational difference is that some power resources that may have been left ON in the S2 state may not be available to the S3 state. As such, some devices may be in a lower-power state when the system is in the S3 state than when the system is in the S2 state. Similarly, some device wake events can function in S2 but not S3.

d. S4: Also known as Hibernation or Suspend to Disk. The S4 sleeping state is the lowest-power, longest wake latency sleeping state supported by ACPI. In order to reduce power to a minimum, it is assumed that the hardware platform has powered off all devices. Because this is a sleeping state, the platform context is maintained. Depending on how the transition into the S4 sleeping state occurs, the responsibility for maintaining system context changes between OSPM and BIOS. To preserve context, in this state all content of the main memory is saved to non-volatile memory such as a hard drive and is powered down. The contents of RAM are restored on resume. All hardware is in the off state and maintains no context.

• G2/S5: Also referred to as Soft Off. In G2/S5, all hardware is in the off state and maintains no context. OSPM places the platform in the S5, soft-off, state to achieve a logical off. The S5 state is not a sleeping state (it is a G2 state), and no context is saved by OSPM or hardware, but power may still be applied to parts of the platform in this state, and as such, it is not safe to take the system apart. Also, from a hardware perspective, the S4 and S5 states are nearly identical. When initiated, the hardware will sequence the system to a state similar to the off state. The hardware has no responsibility for maintaining any system context (memory or I/O); however, it does allow a transition to the S0 state due to a power button press or a remote start.

- G3: Mechanical Off. Same as S5. Additionally, the power supply is isolated. The computer's power has been totally removed via a mechanical switch, and no electrical current is running through. This is the only state that the system can be worked on without damaging the hardware.

Device States

In addition to global and system states, ACPI defines various device states ranging from D0 to D3. The exact definition or meaning of specific device states depends on the device class. A device class describes a type of device – for example, audio, storage, network, and so on:

- D0: This state is assumed to be the highest level of functionality and power consumption. The device is completely active and responsive and is expected to remember all relevant contexts.

- D1: Many device classes may not support D1. In general, D1 is expected to save less power and preserve more device context than D2. D1 may cause the device to lose some context.

- D2: Many device classes may not support D2. In general, D2 is expected to save more power and preserve less device context than D1 or D0. D2 may cause the device to lose some context.

- D3 Hot: Devices in the D3 Hot state are required to be software enumerable. In general, D3 Hot is expected to save more power and optionally preserve device context. If device context is lost when this state is entered, the OS software will reinitialize the device when transitioning back to D0.

- D3 Cold: Power has been fully removed from the device. The device context is lost when this state is entered, so the OS software will have to fully reinitialize the device when powering it back on. Devices in this state have the longest restore times.

Processor States

ACPI defines the power state of system processors while in the G0 working state as being either active (executing) or sleeping (not executing). Processor power states are designated as C0, C1, C2, C3, ... Cn. The C0 power state is an active power state where the CPU executes instructions. The C1–Cn power states are processor sleeping states where the processor consumes less power and dissipates less heat than leaving the processor in the C0 state. While in a sleeping state, the processor does not execute any instructions. Each processor sleeping state has a latency associated with entering and exiting that corresponds to the power savings. In general, the longer the entry/exit latency, the greater the power savings is for the state. To conserve power, OSPM places the processor into one of its supported sleeping states when idle. While in the C0 state, ACPI allows the performance of the processor to be altered through a defined "throttling" process and through transitions into multiple performance states (P states). A diagram of processor power states (not to be confused with performance states) is provided in Figure C-2.

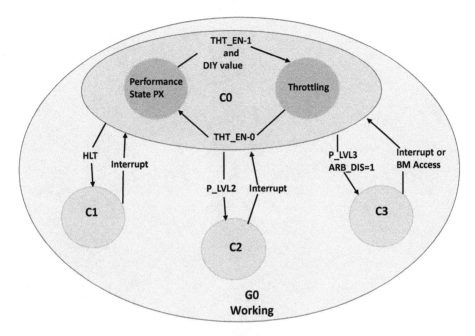

Figure C-2. *Processor Power States*

In summary, one of the main goals of OSPM is to save power/energy when the workload allows it, and detecting inactivity and putting the devices and the system (if possible) in their low-power states forms the heart of power management software.

APPENDIX D

System Boot Flow

When we press the power button on our computing device, we are well aware that the system goes through a bootup process. The boot process culminates with the system being ready for use. But what happens during the boot process is not very well understood widely. In this chapter, we will strive to resolve that.

As shown in Figure D-1, there are four main boot phases on IA devices. The first phase is system hardware bring-up/power-on, which is primarily hardwired to bring up the foundation for software components to get started and take over. Then the BIOS (aka system firmware) phase is responsible for basic initialization and bring-up of system hardware enabling things to pass to the next stage, where the boot loader loads the OS into memory and then begins OS initialization. This last phase takes care of initialization of critical parts of the HW and SW system before making itself available to the user.

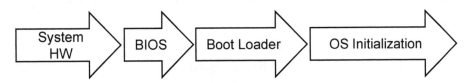

Figure D-1. *High-Level System Boot Flow*

P. D. Crutcher et al., *Essential Computer Science*,
https://doi.org/10.1007/978-1-4842-7107-0

On receiving a "Power Good" signal, CPUs are hardwired to start fetching and executing at a predefined location (address), which is called the "Reset Vector." The Reset Vector points to BIOS code. So, when the CPU is out of reset and starts fetching code from the "Reset Vector," it happens to be BIOS code, which is how BIOS code gets the control and starts executing. Keep in mind that before control comes to CPU and BIOS code, there are a few system hardware- and firmware-related initializations and configurations that happen.

BIOS discovers, enumerates, and initializes the HW devices present. After that it runs power-on self-test (POST). The POST is responsible for validating the sanity of fundamental hardware components. One of the fundamental hardware components in the system happens to be memory. BIOS has a component specialized for memory initialization called the Memory Reference Code (MRC). Another of BIOS's responsibility is to prepare the hardware configuration and memory map and pass those to the OS, in the form of tables. The format and mechanism of information exchange is defined by a standard body, Unified Extensible Firmware Interface (UEFI). Today, most BIOS is UEFI spec compliant. BIOS also adheres to the ACPI specification in passing platform resource(s) information to the OS.

If all goes well, BIOS now identifies a bootable disk and reads the master boot record (MBR) of that disk. The MBR is located in the first sector of the bootable media (could be hard drive, flash, solid-state device, etc.).

The MBR is 512 bytes in size. It has three components: primary boot loader information in the first 446 bytes, partition table in the next 64 bytes, and MBR validation check in the last 2 bytes.

The primary boot loader in the MBR will attempt to locate an active (bootable) partition in the media's partition table. If such a partition is found, the boot sector of that partition is loaded in memory, and then the control jumps to that. Each operating system has its own boot sector format. The boot sector has a small program that locates the OS loader, reads that into memory, and launches that.

The OS loader loads essential system drivers that are required to read data from the disk and initializes the system to the point where the kernel can begin execution.

After OS loading, the OS initialization phase starts. In the OS initialization phase, first, the kernel initialization and plug-and-play activity happen. After that, relevant services are started, and the user interface (could be a command line shell or a full-blown graphical user interface) is presented and the system is now ready for use.

Index

A

© Paul D. Crutcher, Neeraj Kumar Singh, and Peter Tiegs 2021
P. D. Crutcher et al., *Essential Computer Science*,
https://doi.org/10.1007/978-1-4842-7107-0

W, X, Y, Z

FEB   2022